Case Interview Questions for Tech Companies

155 Real Interview Questions and Answers

LEWIS C. LIN

With Teng Lu

ALSO BY LEWIS C. LIN

Decode and Conquer: Answers to Product Management Interviews

Five Minutes to a Better Salary: Over 60 Brilliant Salary Negotiation Scripts for Getting More

Interview Math: Over 50 Problems and Solutions for Quant Case Interview Questions

PM Interview Questions: Over 160 Problems and Solutions for Product Management Interview Questions

Rise Above the Noise: How to Stand Out at the Marketing Interview

Whatever you are, be a good one.
ABRAHAM LINCOLN

Published by Impact Interview, 115 North 85th St., Suite 202, Seattle, WA 98103.

Several fictitious examples have been used in this book; these examples involve names of real people, places and organizations. Any slights of people, places or organizations are unintentional.

The author and publisher have made every effort to ensure the accuracy and completeness of information contained in this book. However, we assume no responsibility for errors, inaccuracies, omissions or any inconsistency herein. This book is sold without warranty, either expressed or implied. Neither the authors, the publishers, distributors or other affiliates will be held liable for any damages caused either directly or indirectly by the instructions contained in this book.

This book uses trademarked names in an editorial fashion and to the benefit of the trademark owner, with no intention of infringement of the trademark. Hence we do not indicate every occurrence of a trademarked name.

Corporations, organizations and educational institutions: bulk quantity pricing is available. For information, contact lewis@impactinterview.com.

FIRST EDITION / Second Printing

Lin, Lewis C.
Case Interview Questions for Tech Companies: 155 Real Interview Questions and Answers / Lewis C. Lin.

Table of Contents

Chapter 1 Introduction
What are case interview questions?

Congratulations on concentrating your job hunt on technology companies like Google, Amazon, Apple and Uber. If you picked up this book, you are likely interviewing for the roles below:

- Product management
- Marketing
- Operations
- Finance
- Strategy
- Business Development

At the interview, it is very possible that you will get case interview questions. Case questions are different from traditional and behavioral interview questions like:

- Tell me about yourself. And why do you want to join our company?
- Tell me a time when you persuaded executives to build a product feature they did not want to build.

Case questions are interview questions about a hypothetical business situation or case. They are meant to test how one would approach and solve that business problem. Here are some examples, reported by candidates:

Role	Company	Question
Product management	Google	Estimate how much Gmail costs per user, per year.
Product management	Google	Improve the Disneyland user experience, relevant to a Google product.
Pathways & operations management	Amazon	During the holiday season, Amazon customers shipped 200 orders per second. Amazon's data science team discovered that the average number of orders waiting to be shipped was 20,650. How long did the average Amazon order wait to be shipped?
Global supply management	Apple	Describe how supply chain works for Apple. What challenges do we face on a day-to-day basis?
Business development	Coursera	As a Coursera business development executive, how would you manage to build relationships with school administrators?
Marketing management	Microsoft	Create a marketing campaign for Microsoft Office 365.
Marketing intelligence & business analytics	Facebook	Which is better? Having 10 false positives or 80 false positives?
Finance	Amazon	How would you reprice Amazon Prime if your goal was to increase profitability?
Corporate strategy	Microsoft	How would you reposition Google's offerings to counteract competitive threats from Microsoft?

Welcome to the world of case questions for the tech industry. These questions can stun both novices and experts alike. If you are interviewing for a business role at a tech company, whether it's product management, marketing, operations or finance, you need to be ready for case questions.

Origin of case questions

Management consulting firms, like McKinsey & Company, popularized case questions. Consulting case questions simulate a client engagement. The interviewer would play the role of the client or facilitator; the candidate would play the role of a consultant. The aspiring consultant would answer the question by:

- Listening to the client's description of a business problem
- Asking clarifying questions
- Presenting a hypothesis
- Analyzing facts and data, to confirm or deny the hypothesis
- Brainstorming solutions
- Making a final recommendation

Why interviewers ask case questions

Consulting firms deemed traditional interview questions ineffective in appraising a candidate's problem solving skills, so they invented the case interview. Happy with the results, consulting firms have made case interviews a permanent fixture in their candidate evaluation processes. And the tech industry, stuffed with ex-McKinsey consultants, have embraced consulting's case interview tradition.

To summarize, case questions, in any industry, are meant to evaluate a candidate's:

- Problem solving skills
- Communication skills
- Business judgment
- Courage and impact when making a recommendation

Effectiveness in in evaluating a candidate's ability

The case interview can be considered a work simulation since it simulates what candidates might be asked to do on the job. Work simulations (and work sample tests) seem to indicate a candidate's potential. Two employment testing experts, Frank Schmidt and John Hunter, concluded that work sample tests are indeed the best way to determine one's candidacy. Their research shows that work sample tests outperformed the next best method, structured interviews, in evaluating candidates by six percent.

How case questions for tech companies differ from consulting

Case questions at consulting and tech firms have many similarities including:

- Ask candidates to solve business problems

11

- Require candidates to have a methodical approach
- Typically call for number crunching
- Expect candidates to make a recommendation, affecting the target goal in an effective and logical way

However, unlike consulting case questions, tech case questions are more likely to have the following characteristics:

- **Involve real-world scenarios.** To maintain client privacy, consulting cases often use fictitious company names and scenarios. Tech firms are more likely to use actual problems, making case questions easier to anticipate.
- **Be ambiguous.** Tech companies use questions that are less specific and more open-ended, similar to the broad strategic questions that tech CEOs face day-to-day.
- **Require tech domain-expertise.** Consulting firms don't expect candidates have industry-specific knowledge, but tech firms do.
- **Dearth of background information.** Unlike consulting cases, tech cases rarely, if ever, have background information to share with the candidate. There is no interview guide, and the interviewer usually do not have exhibits to reveal to the interviewee.
- **Unlikely to provide clues, help or other assistance.** Consulting interviewers often help candidates with unknown assumptions. Tech companies are less helpful in this regard. Sometimes, they don't know or don't want to reveal company confidential information. Other times, they withhold assumptions so they can assess a candidate's judgment.

What the book is about and how to use it

This book includes over 150 practice problems along with sample answers. The questions are organized by question type; there are different question categories including product design, marketing, operations, finance and business development.

The best candidates are attempting the problems on their own and then comparing their answers with the sample. I would strongly recommend that you do the same.

To reinforce that concept, I created blank pages for the first 10 questions. After that, I hope you continue to do problems first and then review the sample answer.

And one more tip: do your research on the types of questions you're likely to encounter; pick and choose the sample questions that are most similar to what you think you're likely to get at the actual interview.

Who should read this book

If you are interviewing for any of the following roles at tech companies, you should be prepared for case interview questions:

- Product management
- Operations

- Business Development
- Marketing
- Finance
- Strategy

Why I'm confident you'll get better

In 2015, I released a similar book called, *Interview Math: Over 50 Problems and Solutions for Quant Case Interview Questions*. It's targeted to aspiring management consultants applying at top-tier firms like McKinsey, Bain and Boston Consulting Group. It included estimation, profitability, breakeven and pricing questions.

As readers made their way through every problem, they gained remarkable proficiency, including readers who believed or were told they were not born to do math.

With *Case Interview Questions*, you'll be empowered in the same way. You may be terrified of product design, metrics and technical interview questions now. And that's normal. We do not practice these interview questions every day. But I'm positive that if you dedicate yourself, you'll see a significant 10 to 15X improvement in your PM interview skills.

Have these books and frameworks within an arm's reach

Many of you have read my previous books. This book has brand new questions and sample answers. Here's a list of books that you'll want to have within an arm's reach:

- *Decode and Conquer* has explanations to PM-related frameworks including the CIRCLES™ Method, AARM™ and DIGS™.
- *Rise Above the Noise* has explanations to marketing-related frameworks including the Big Picture Framework, MOB and important pricing frameworks.
- *Interview Math* has great introductory material and provides more methods on how to tackle estimation, market sizing, ROI and lifetime value questions, especially if you find the harder analytical questions in this book too intimidating.

Lastly, if you're a product management candidate looking for even more practice questions and sample answers, grab a copy of my book *PM Interview Questions*, where you'll find another 160+ practice questions.

Email me

I'd love to hear your feedback, comments and even typos. Contact me at lewis@impactinterview.com.

Lewis C. Lin
March 2017

Chapter 2 Finding Practice Partners and Bonus Resources

I created a community of practice partners so that you can get feedback on your interview responses. And to accompany your partner practice, I've created interview evaluation sheets too.

Find Practice Partners

Practicing with others is incredibly beneficial. It will:

- Give you a fresh perspective
- Provide moral support
- Keep you accountable

Finding practice partners is not easy, so I created a special Slack community for all of you. Type bit.ly/InterviewPartner into your Internet browser to join:

Here's what people have said about our mock interview practice partner communities:

"Thanks to this community, I have found partners and am getting a fair bit of practice in." – M.A.

"Hey Lewis, you already know this, but you've built something amazing here. I've done a few practice interviews now and most folks have been welcoming and really helpful. You should be proud ☺ Congrats." – S.G.

"Hey Lewis, awesome group you got going here! A few of us loved your presentation at Berkeley Haas this past weekend and will be using your resources to get a few study groups together to work on cases. Looking forward to interacting with everyone here." – J.Z.

Interview Evaluation Sheets

We tend to improve quickly when we have clear, actionable feedback. To help you get that feedback, I've created interview evaluation sheets that your practice partner can fill out.

The evaluation sheets contain criteria that hiring managers look for in top-notch interview responses. It is based off of my research with hiring managers on how they evaluate product management, operations, strategy, finance and business development candidates.

Interview Evaluation Sheet: Product Design

Downloadable copy for printing: bit.ly/InterviewEvalProductDesign

	Rating 1-5 1 = Not like the candidate at all 5 = Very much like the candidate	Interviewer's Explanation
Goals & Metrics Did the candidate define objectives before answering? Were the candidate's selections reasonable?		
Target Persona & Pain Points Did the candidate choose a target persona? Did the candidate explain the persona's pain points to the extent that demonstrated true consumer insight?		
Prioritization Did the candidate demonstrate ability to prioritize competing use cases or pain points in a compelling way?		
Creativity Did the candidate demonstrate sufficient creativity? Or were the ideas copycats of competitive features and products?		
Development Leadership When asked, did the candidate have a reasonable explanation on how a proposed feature would be implemented?		
Summary and Next Steps Did the candidate summarize their main argument at the end, including clear next steps?		

Interview Evaluation Sheet: Estimation

	Rating 1-5 1 = Not like the candidate at all 5 = Very much like the candidate	Interviewer's Explanation
Problem Solving Skills Did the candidate take an unfamiliar problem and develop a plan to solve it confidently?		
Communication Skills Did the candidate clearly communicate his or her action plan to the interviewer? Easy-to-follow? Or did the interviewer have to ask an excessive number of clarifying questions to unravel the candidate's thoughts?		
Comfort with Numbers Did the candidate confidently calculate numbers by hand? Or was the candidate hesitant? Did the candidate rely on using a calculator or computer to crunch numbers? Or did the candidate needlessly round numbers to oversimplify calculations?		
Judgment Did the candidate choose reasonable assumptions, backed by logical thinking? Or was the candidate sloppy in choosing assumptions, believing that reasonable assumptions don't matter?		

Interview Evaluation Sheet: Metrics

	Rating 1-5 1 = Not like the candidate at all 5 = Very much like the candidate	Interviewer's Explanation
Understanding Metrics Did the candidate have an understanding of product metrics? Did the candidate provide a comprehensive and relevant list?		
Evaluating Metrics Did the candidate articulate which metrics are better than others, backed with sound logic and evidence?		
Diagnosing Metrics How was the candidate's diagnosis? Did the candidate provide an issue tree depicting drivers that affect that specific metric?		
Affecting Change on a Metric Did the candidate offer a plan on how to positively influence a metric, primarily through product changes but perhaps through other levers, including marketing and business development initiatives?		

Interview Evaluation Sheet: Behavioral

Downloadable copy for printing: bit.ly/InterviewEvalBehavioral

	Rating 1-5 1 = Not like the candidate at all 5 = Very much like the candidate	Interviewer's Explanation
Owner vs. Participant Did the candidate play a primary or marginal role?		
Good vs. Great Achievement Was the achievement impressive? Were the results largely due to the candidate's impact? Or would the results have occurred, even without the candidate's involvement?		
Communication Skills Is the candidate's story easy-to-follow and memorable? Was it a struggle to extract information from the candidate?		

Interview Evaluation Sheet: Strategy

	Rating 1-5 1 = Not like the candidate at all 5 = Very much like the candidate	Interviewer's Explanation
Customer-Focused Did the candidate include an exploration of customers in the strategic discussion?		
Diagnosing the Business Does the candidate understand the business model? Did the candidate surgically diagnose problems, quickly and effectively?		
Solutions Were the candidate solutions specific to the problem at hand? Was it appropriate for the company's business model and target customer? Are the recommendations innovative or simply copycat?		

Interview Evaluation Sheet: Operations

Downloadable copy for printing: bit.ly/InterviewEvalOperations

	Rating 1-5 1 = Not like the candidate at all 5 = Very much like the candidate	**Interviewer's Explanation**
Objective Did the candidate define an appropriate objective or problem statement?		
Business Drivers Did the candidate identify the relevant business drivers for the goal or problem?		
Solutions Are the solutions creative? Do they address specific business drivers that make measurable impact?		

Interview Evaluation Sheet: Finance

	Rating 1-5 1 = Not like the candidate at all 5 = Very much like the candidate	Interviewer's Explanation
Financial Knowledge Does the candidate demonstrate understanding and mastery of financial concepts? Can the candidate explain concepts to others?		
Analytical Ability Is the candidate comfortable making calculations?		
Communication Skills Can the candidate explain complex financial concepts in an easy-to-understand manner?		
Strategic Insight Can the candidate connect their financial analysis with business strategy? Does the analysis recommend a specific decision or course of action?		

Interview Evaluation Sheet: Marketing

Downloadable copy for printing: bit.ly/InterviewEvalMarketing

	Rating 1-5 1 = Not like the candidate at all 5 = Very much like the candidate	Interviewer's Explanation
Business Judgment Did the candidate specify a goal? Is it appropriate for the company's situation?		
Strategic Thinking Did the candidate specify a marketing strategy including a discussion of target segments and value proposition?		
Tactical Creativity Did the tactics demonstrate creativity? Are they in line with the marketing strategy and goal? Does the candidate convey understanding of how to execute each tactic?		
Business Impact Did the proposed marketing plan appear reasonable in meeting the goal?		

Interview Evaluation Sheet: Business Development

	Rating 1-5 1 = Not like the candidate at all 5 = Very much like the candidate	Interviewer's Explanation
Problem Clarification Did the candidate clarify the issue and ask appropriate questions?		
Gap Identification Did the candidate methodically investigate the root cause of the problem?		
Brainstorming Skills Did the candidate brainstorm several alternatives to the problem?		
Business Judgment Did the candidate recommend a single, reasonable solution for the situation?		

Interview Evaluation Sheet: Other Question Types

Downloadable copy for printing: bit.ly/InterviewEvalOther

	Rating 1-5 1 = Not like the candidate at all 5 = Very much like the candidate	Interviewer's Explanation
Communication Skills Did the candidate provide a response that is well-organized and easy-to-follow? Or was it boring and disorganized?		
Critical Thinking & Insights Did the candidate provide thought-provoking insights? Did you feel smarter after talking to the candidate?		
Creativity Did the candidate show vision and imagination?		
Problem Solving Skills Did the candidate take an unfamiliar, unambiguous question, problem or situation and provide a plan as well as compelling leadership?		

Chapter 3 Abbreviations, Terms and Concepts

Abbreviations

This book will deal with large numbers in the thousands, millions and billions. To save space, I will use the following abbreviations:

- K = thousands
- M = millions
- B = billions

For instance, 10K refers to 10,000. 10M is equivalent to 10,000,000, and 10B is equivalent to 10,000,000,000.

I will also use these shorthand abbreviations:

- Q = quantity
- P = price
- R = revenue
- C = cost

Terms and Concepts

AARM metrics™

An analytical framework that defines the metrics for a product.

- **Acquisition:** Tracking customer signups for a service. The bar for signing up for a service has gotten lower and lower, thanks to the popularity of free signup and pay later "freemium" models. The typical metric to track here is lazy registrations.
- **Activation:** Getting users that have completed a lazy registration to fully register. For a social networking site like Google+, this may include uploading a photo or completing their profile page.
- **Retention:** Getting users to use the service often and behave in a way that helps the user or business. Key metrics include adding more information to their profile page, checking the news feed frequently or inviting friends to try the service.
- **Monetization:** Collecting revenue from users. It could include the number of people who are paying for the service or the average revenue per user (ARPU).

A/B Testing

A product decision-making method by comparing results between two different versions of a web page or related user experience.

Agile Development

A product development method to develop products incrementally to incorporate customer feedback. It's the opposite of waterfall development where all the features are specified in the beginning.

Before and After Analysis

A way to interview answers to consider the before and after impact of a change.

Big Picture Framework

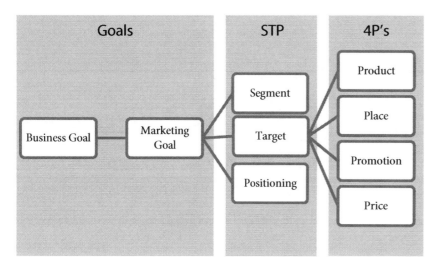

A comprehensive model that provides an effective way to answer interview questions about marketing plans and campaigns. There are three parts to the framework: Goals, STP (segmentation, targeting, and positioning) and the 4P's (product, place, promotion, and price).

- Goals: State the overall business objective and intermediate marketing objectives that contribute to it.
- Segmentation: Group buyers by attributes to identify customers that would benefit from the product.
- Targeting: Choose segments that would appreciate and seek out the product's benefits.
- Positioning: Create a product image for customer segments through the 4P's.
- Product: Develop new product ideas using the CIRCLES Method.
- Place: Choose the distribution channel that best meets the business goal(s).
- Promotion: Match promotional tactics with your strategies.
- Price: Use breakeven analysis for existing products, and the pricing meter for new products.

CIRCLES Method™

A guideline that provides complete and thoughtful responses to product design questions.

- **Comprehend the Situation:** Avoid miscommunication by asking clarifying questions (5W's and H) and/or stating assumptions.
- **Identify the Customer:** List potential customer personas, and choose one to focus on.
- **Report the Customer's Needs:** Provide a user story that conveys their goals, desires, and potential benefits. *As a <role>, I want <goal/desire> so that <benefit>.*
- **Cut, Through Prioritization:** Showcase your ability to prioritize, assess tradeoffs, and make decisions. Create a prioritization matrix that estimates valuable metrics (revenue, customer satisfaction, etc.)

- List Solutions: Brainstorm at least three BIG ideas that exploit future trends in technology and customer behavior. Use the following frameworks for inspiration: 1) Reverse the situation to uncover new possibilities. 2) Mix and match product attributes to get new combinations. 3) Challenge the status quo.
- Evaluate Tradeoffs: Define your tradeoff criteria and analyze the solution through a pro and cons list.
- Summarize Your Recommendation: Specify which product or feature you'd recommend, recap its benefits to the user and/or company, and explain why you preferred this solution compared to others.

Cohort analysis

Measure and compare differences of a specific customer segment, over time.

Critical Path Dependency

A strategic relationship between a preceding and succeeding task in a sequence of activities that impacts the project end date. Predecessor tasks must be finished before the start of successor tasks.

DIGS Method™

To get a job offer, I believe that candidates have to do just two things: be likable and show credibility that they can do the job. DIGS Method™ is a behavioral interview framework that promotes credibility and likability in your response.

- **D**ramatize the situation: Provide context and details that emphasizes the importance of your job, project or product.
- **I**ndicate the alternatives: Be thoughtful and analytical by listing three different approaches to a problem.
- **G**o through what you did: Convince the listener that you were the driving force.
- **S**ummarize your impact: Provide numbers and qualitative statements that validate your impact.

5Es Framework

An acronym to help brainstorm different stages of the customer experience. In other words, use this framework to quickly and easily build a customer journey map. Here are the 5Es:

- Entice. What event triggers a user to enter into the UX funnel?
- Enter. What's the first few steps in the UX funnel?
- Engage. What task(s) is the user trying to accomplish?
- Exit. How does the user complete the task?
- Extend. What follow-up actions occur after the user completes the task?

A customer journey map can help one more effectively answer product design questions.

Five Ws and H

A checklist of questions to get the complete facts on a situation. For example, when understanding a new product, here's what listeners want to know:

- **W**hat is it?
- **W**ho is it for?

- **W**hen is it ready?
- **W**here will it be available?
- **W**hy should I get it?
- **H**ow does it work?

Five Whys

A technique to determine cause of a particular situation. It involves asking "Why?" in succession.

Issue Trees

A problem-solving diagram that breaks down a 'Why' or 'How' question into identifiable root causes or potential solutions, respectively.

Marketing funnel

An analytical model that tracks the customer journey towards a purchase of a product or service. There are four general steps, indicated by the AITP acronym:

- **A**wareness: Bring recognition to a product brand.
- **I**nterest: Stir fascination with a product (what it does, how it works, and what benefit it delivers.)
- **T**rial: Compel a prospective user to try the product.
- **P**urchase: Get the customer to buy into the product.

Minimum Viable Product (MVP)

The minimum set of features to gather user feedback for a product concept. It can be a fully functioning product, or it can be simply sketches on a piece of paper.

MOB

A marketing framework that evaluates the effectiveness of a product advertisement or commercial.

- **M**emorable: Does the ad grab your attention? Is it worthy of future discussion with your friends, acquaintances and social media?
- **O**h, Product!: Is the product and brand promoted clearly and definitively?
- **B**enefit: Does the ad explain and provide evidence for a product's benefit? Is there a clear reason why the consumer should choose the product over a competitor's?

Rule of Three

A communication principle that suggests that responses that are bundled in threes are more effective and satisfying.

Personas

A representation of a group of customers, defined by their goals and objectives. Detailed personas can be described in terms of an example representative's demographics, psychographics and behavior.

Pro and Con Analysis

A communication principle that a particular point of view is more readily accepted if the speaker provides a balanced view, in other words both the advantages and disadvantages.

Porter's Five Forces

A model proposed by Harvard business school professor, Michael Porter, on the competitive forces affecting a product or service. Here are the key components of Porter's Five Forces:

- Threat of new entrants
- Threat of substitutes
- Bargaining power of buyers
- Bargaining power of suppliers
- Industry rivalry

Razor-and-Razorblade Strategy

A popular business strategy where a business sells the platform, such as a razor, at cost or less. Then the business sells complementary products, such as razorblades, at a substantial profit, offsetting the reduced profit from selling the platform.

Root Cause Analysis Tree

A hierarchical diagram that identifies the root causes of a problem and provides potential corrective actions to benefit the outcome or prevent recurrence.

SCAMPER

A creative thinking framework used to develop innovative ideas for a topic, product or service.

- **S**ubstitute: What components of the topic can be substituted?
- **C**ombine: What ideas, products or services can be added to the original topic?
- **A**djust: How can the topic be altered to be more flexible and adaptable?
- **M**odify: What components can be enhanced, reduced or changed?
- **P**ut to other uses: How can the topic, product or service be used in different scenarios or situations?
- **E**liminate: What ideas or components can be removed?
- **R**everse, Rearrange: What new approaches can be formed from the original topic?

SMART Goals

A helpful framework for metrics questions, especially when identifying the most important metric. The SMART acronym has many variations, which I've included here:

- **S**: specific, significant, stretching
- **M**: measurable, meaningful, motivational
- **A**: agreed upon, attainable, achievable, acceptable, action-oriented
- **R**: realistic, relevant, reasonable, rewarding, results-oriented

- **T**: time-based, time-bound, timely, tangible, trackable

SWOT Analysis

A structured planning method to evaluate the strategic elements of a business, industry or product to find its competitive advantage.

- **S**trengths: Attributes that provide an advantage over other competitors.
- **W**eaknesses: Attributes that provide a disadvantage relative to other competitors.
- **O**pportunities: Elements that can be utilized to maximize advantages or trends.
- **T**hreats: Elements in the environment that can be an obstacle or risk to your business or product.

Viral Loop

Similar to word-of-mouth marketing, getting users in the process of referring others to use a product or service.

Waterfall Development

A product development method where all the features are specified in the beginning. This is the opposite of Agile development where the product development is developed incrementally to allow for incorporation of customer feedback.

Chapter 4 Analytics: Estimation

Free WiFi

Estimate how much it will cost to deliver free WiFi to all of San Francisco?

Show your work below. Make any assumptions as necessary. Answer on the next page.

Answer

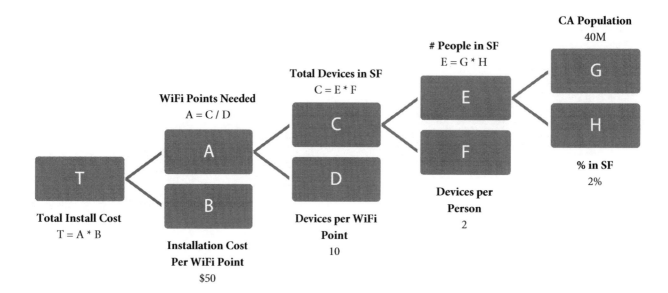

Clarifications

Installation cost, not monthly cost.

Calculations

$E = 40M * 2\% = 800K$

$C = 800K * 2 = 1.6M$

$A = 1.6M / 10 = 160K$

Answer

$T = 160K * \$50 = \$8M$

Lotion Bottles

How many lotion bottles are produced in the US each year?

Show your work below. Make any assumptions as necessary. Answer on the next page.

Answer

Assumptions

- All types of body lotion, including special varieties for babies or older people.
- Production is the same as consumption. It's true that some bottles made from Q4 last year would be used in Q1 this year, but bottles would be made in Q4 this year for Q1 next year.
- 300 million people in the US.
- 75% of people use lotion once per day.
- 15% of people use lotion once per two days.
- 5% of people use lotion once per week.
- 5% of people don't use lotion.
- A typical lotion bottle is about 1 liter.
- It takes about 6 months, so 60 x 3 = 120 uses to use the whole thing up. That means it must be replaced every 120 uses.

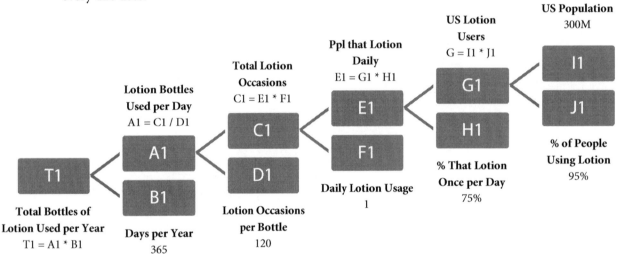

Calculations T1

$G1 = 300M * 95\% = 285M$

$E1 = 285M * 75\% = 213.75M$

$C1 = 213.75M * 1 = 213.75M$

$A1 = 213.75M / 120 = 1.781M$

Sub-Answer T1

$T1 = 1.781M * 365 = 650.156M$

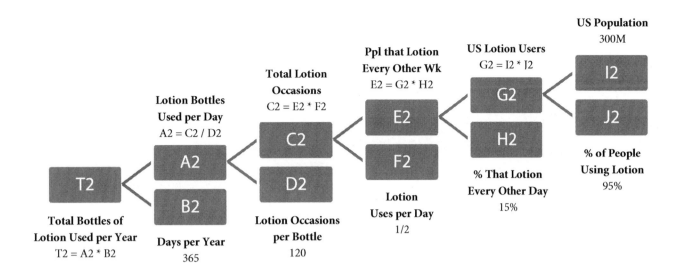

Calculations T2

$G2 = 300M * 95\% = 285M$

$E2 = 285M * 15\% = 42.75M$

$C2 = 42.75M * /2 = 21.375M$

$A2 = 21.375M / 120 = 178.1K$

Sub-Answer T2

$T2 = 178.1K * 365 = 65.0M$

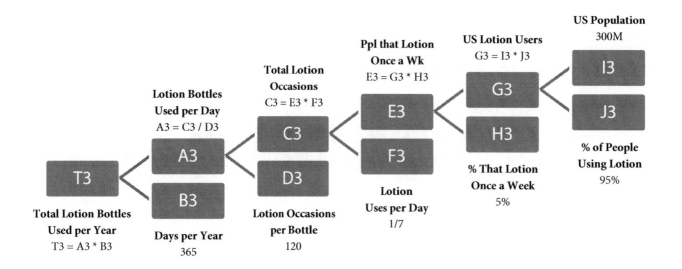

Calculations T3

$G3 = 300M * 95\% = 285M$

$E3 = 285M * 5\% = 14.25M$

$C3 = 14.25M * 1/7 = 2.0357M$

$A3 = 2.0357M / 120 = 16.98K$

Sub-Answer T3

$T3 = 16.98K * 365 = 6.20M$

Total Answer

$T = T1 + T2 + T3 = 650.156M + 65.0M + 6.20M = {\sim}721.356M$

Printers Sold Annually

How many printers are sold each year?

Show your work below. Make any assumptions as necessary. Answer on the next page.

Answer

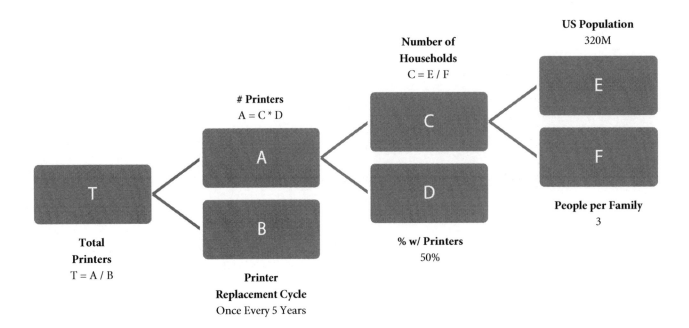

Assumptions

- United States only
- Home printers only
- Printers sold to existing printer owners, not including those who want to buy a printer but don't already have one

Calculations

C: 320M / 3 = 106.7M

A = 106.7 * 50% = 53.3M

Answer

T = 53.3 / 5 = 10.7M

Number of Buses Owned

How many buses do the local corporate bus companies own?

Show your work below. Make any assumptions as necessary. Answer on the next page.

Answer

Assumptions

- About 2 million people in the Bay Area.
- Buses run from 7 AM to 12 AM. That's 17 hours.
- Rush hour (almost always full) from 7 AM to 9 AM, 11 AM to 1 PM, and 5 PM to 8 PM. That's a total of 7 hours of rush hour.
- During rush hours, the buses run every 30 minutes instead of every hour.
- An average full route of the bus takes about an hour.
- There are probably around 30 routes for buses.
- About 50 people per bus (40 seats and 10 standing up).
- Only about 15% of the people ride buses.

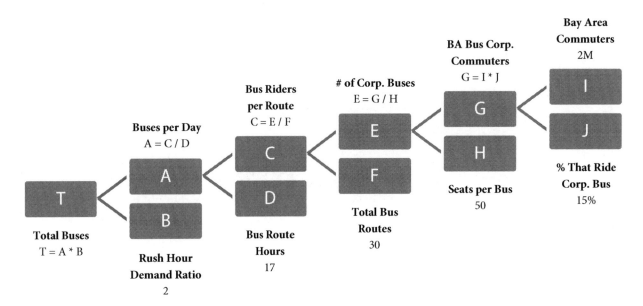

Calculations

G = 2M * 15% = 300K

E = 300K / 50 = 6K

C = 6K / 30 = 200

A = 200 / 17 = ~12

Answer

T = 12 * 2 = 24

Uber Cars per Hour

If 1,000 people opened the Uber app during one hour, how many cars do you need?

Show your work below. Make any assumptions as necessary. Answer on the next page.

Answer

CANDIDATE: Is this during regular hours, rush hours or some inactive hours like 4AM?

INTERVIEWER: This is at 10AM.

CANDIDATE: What day is this?

INTERVIEWER: Monday.

CANDIDATE: Do you want to know how many cars I need on the road for this one hour, this day or this week? What mean is, should I take into account the whole day, the whole week or just this one hour?

INTERVIEWER: You should take the whole week into account.

CANDIDATE: I can estimate how many cars I need, but I do want to point out since Uber drivers are not obligated to show up, they usually take into account rush hours and weekdays vs. weekends. What we can do is increase their rates to incentivize them to show up, but it's not a 100% guarantee.

INTERVIEWER: That's fine.

CANDIDATE: Okay, then I would make some assumptions:

- Rush hour is morning (7-9AM), lunch (12–1PM), and dinner (5-7PM) during the weekdays.
- Weekend rush hour would include late-night (12-2AM).
- Rush hour would probably see a 100% increase in traffic.
- Weekend would probably see an increase traffic of 50%.

Let's plug all of this into a formula:

Calculating cars for the weekday

$$Weekday\ Cars = Normal\ Hours * People\ per\ Hour * (1 + \frac{Rush\ Hours}{Hours\ per\ Day})$$

$$Weekday\ Cars = 19 * 1,000 * (1 + \frac{5}{24})$$

$$Weekday\ Cars = {\sim}23,000$$

Calculating cars for the weekend

$$Weekend\ Cars = Normal\ Hours * People\ per\ Hour * Weekend\ Bonus * (1 + \frac{Rush\ Hours}{Hours\ per\ Day})$$

$$Weekend\ Cars = 17 * 1,000 * 2 * (1 + \frac{7}{24})$$

$$Weekend\ Cars = {\sim}44,000$$

Calculating cars for the whole week

$$Weekly\ Cars = \#\ Weekdays * Weekday\ Cars + \#\ Weekend\ Days * Weekend\ Cars$$

$$Weekly\ Cars = 5 * 23{,}000 + 2 * 44{,}000$$

$$Weekly\ Cars = 203{,}000$$

Average cars per hour

$$Average\ Cars\ per\ Hour = \frac{Weekly\ Cars}{Days\ per\ Week * Hours\ per\ Day}$$

$$Average\ Cars\ per\ Hour = \frac{203{,}000}{7 * 24}$$

$$Average\ Cars\ per\ Hour = \sim 1{,}200$$

CANDIDATE: I say we need about 1200 cars per hour on average.

Google Glass' Market Value

How do you evaluate Google Glass' market value?

Things to Consider

- Did you consider the benefit that a user might get from using Google Glass?
- To save time, did you constrain your analysis to a single segment?
- Did you do a back-of-the-envelope market estimate, if required by the interviewer?

Common Mistakes

- Not justifying assumptions
- Giving calculations that's hard to follow

Show your work below. Make any assumptions as necessary. Answer on the next page.

Answer

CANDIDATE: I would evaluate this by picking a persona to focus on. I am thinking these people would find it useful. This list is nowhere near exhaustive:

- Surgeons
- Executives
- Hikers
- Product Managers

Which one do you want me to focus on? I think the PM case is interesting.

INTERVIEWER: That is interesting. Tell me more about the product manager.

CANDIDATE: There are certain use cases:

- **Check task list.** Always check task lists on the go.
- **Stay updated on emails.** If someone sends an email, you'll automatically see it. No need to look at it on the phone.
- **Keep up to schedule.** A PM is always busy, so having a schedule ready is important.
- **Keep up to date.** The PM always needs to keep up-to-date with the latest trends and news, especially about competitors. This lets the PM do this on the go.

These are the cases I am thinking of. Is there one you would like me to focus on?

INTERVIEWER: Which one do you feel is the most important for a PM?

CANDIDATE: Probably staying updated on emails. I know the smartphone is nice and all, but sometimes the PM is too busy (driving, eating, jogging, etc.) to pull out his phone. If his team sends something, it's important for him or her to at least takes a look to avoid a bottleneck.

INTERVIEWER: How would you evaluate the market value for the PM?

CANDIDATE: Well, I would calculate how many PMs there are. I know that the typical PM to engineer ratio is about one to ten. The Bay Area has about two million residents, and I would say at least 20% of those are engineers. So we got about 400K engineers. Los Angeles, Seattle, Texas, New York, and Atlanta are the other major tech cities, but they don't have as many engineers as we do. A rough estimate would be around 1.5 million engineers in the US. I think I'll just calculate the market value in the US, and double it, since companies like Google usually get 50% of their revenue from the US alone.

With 1.5 million engineers, we are looking at 150K PMs. I think the adoption rate would be about 20%. Most PMs are technology lovers, and Google is the mecca for techies. We are looking at 30K Google Glasses for the PMs.

I think each Google Glass costs about $500? So we are looking at $15 million from just PMs alone. That's monetary. We also need to factor the cool factor of owning one.

Normally I'd adjust my estimate for competitive purchases; however, I don't know of any competition to the Google Glass right now.

To conclude, my estimate is $15 million, not counting non-monetary benefits such as word-of-mouth marketing.

Yahoo's Net Income Percentage

Estimate Yahoo's net income percentage.

Things to Consider

- Ask or verify the net income percentage definition so that you are on the same page as the interviewer.
- Think about all the different revenue drivers of Yahoo's business including ad and enterprise sales.
- Don't forget about operational costs.

Common Mistakes

- Not wanting to answer because one is not familiar with the net income definition.
- Think that the interviewer wants to understand the process for finding this information vs. giving an estimate.
- Blurting out an unsubstantiated guess without rationale or calculations.

Show your work below. Make any assumptions as necessary. Answer on the next page.

Answer

Clarifications

- Net income percentage means, how much of total revenue is net profit.

Assumptions

- Yahoo makes money through three channels: ads (Yahoo Search, News, Blogs), Enterprise (Yahoo Mail), and sales (Yahoo Shopping, Yahoo TV)
- Ads probably make up about 75% of Yahoo's revenue. Most of Yahoo's businesses offer content, so ads must be the biggest slice.
- Enterprise probably makes up about 10% of Yahoo's revenue. Yahoo doesn't have that many enterprise products.
- Sales probably makes up about 15% of Yahoo's revenue. Yahoo has a lot of products that focus around sales.
- Google has about 3 billion users worldwide. Yahoo is behind Google, so probably about 1 billion users. The majority of these will be ads.
- A typical user uses some form of Yahoo service at least 4 times a day, and will see about 16 ads (4 each).
- CPC: $1
- CTR: 0.001
- CPM = CPC * CTR * 1000 = $1
- Enterprise differs on pricing and types, but should charge around $10 dollars per user per month.
- Sales really differs on pricing, but again, average. It should be around $200 per user.
- Profit margin is around 50%.
- About 60,000 employees in Yahoo.
- The average salary in Yahoo is around $100,000.
- Office cost and everything should be an additional 10% in salary cost.

Calculations

Calculating Ad Revenue

$$Ad\ Revenue = \ Users * \%\ Ads * CPC * CTR * Ads\ per\ Day * Days\ in\ a\ Year$$

$$Ad\ Revenue = \ 1\ billion * 0.75 * \$1 * 0.001 * 16 * 365$$

$$Ad\ Revenue = \$4.38\ billion$$

Calculating Enterprise Revenue

$$Enterprise\ Revenue = Users * \%\ Enterprise * Cost\ per\ Enterprise\ User * Months\ in\ a\ Year$$

$$Enterprise\ Revenue = 1\ billion * 0.1 * \$10 * 12$$

$$Enterprise\ Revenue = \$12\ billion$$

Calculating Sales Revenue

$$Sales\ Revenue = Users * \%\ Sales * Cost\ per\ Sales\ User$$

$$Sales\ Revenue = 1\ billion * 0.15 * \$200$$

$$Sales\ Revenue = \$30\ billion$$

Calculating Total Revenue

$$Total\ Revenue = Ad\ Revenue + Enterprise\ Revenue + Sales\ Revenue$$

$$Total\ Revenue = \$4.38\ billion + \$12\ billion + \$30\ billion$$

$$Total\ Revenue = \$46.38\ billion$$

Calculating Operating Cost

$$Operating\ Cost = \#\ Employees * Average\ Salary * Office\ Cost$$

$$Operating\ Cost = 60,000 * \$100,000 * 1.1$$

$$Operating\ Cost = \$6.6\ billion$$

Calculating Net Profit

$$Net\ Profit = Total\ Revenue * Profit\ Margin - Operation\ Cost$$

$$Net\ Profit = \$46.38\ billion * 0.5 - \$6.6\ billion$$

$$Net\ Profit = \$16.6\ billion$$

Calculating Net Income Percentage

$$Net\ Income\ Percentage = 100 * \frac{Net\ Profit}{Total\ Revenue}$$

$$Net\ Income\ Percentage = 100 * \frac{\$16.6\ billion}{\$46.38\ billion}$$

Answer

$$Net\ Income\ Percentage = 35.8\%$$

Chapter 5 Analytics: Pricing Existing Products

Repricing Amazon Prime

How would you reprice Amazon Prime if your goal was to increase profitability?

Things to Consider

- Profit = revenue – cost.
- Revenue = price * quantity.
- Cost = fixed cost + (variable cost * quantity)

Common Mistakes

- Fixating on price changes only.
- Not considering how costs can be reduced.
- Factoring only impact on new Prime customers and not existing Prime customers.

Show your work below. Make any assumptions as necessary. Answer on the next page.

This is the last time I'll prompt you to show your work. Keep up the good practice. And no peeking at the answer; sample answers are reserved for finishers!

Answer

CANDIDATE: I need to first think about how Amazon Prime works. So let's recap. Whenever someone purchases something on Amazon, unless he paid $35 and are purchasing eligible items, he will not get free shipping. Even if he does, he only gets five to eight day shipping. Amazon probably takes a loss of $5 or so such on shipping.

If he has Amazon Prime, he has to pay $99 a year, and he gets free two-day shipping on eligible items. How much does two-day shipping cost Amazon?

INTERVIEWER: Around $12.

CANDIDATE: How much does it cost for super saver shipping?

INTERVIEWER: Around $2.

CANDIDATE: Okay, so then I have to make some assumptions:

- There are around 100 million yearly active users. This is a number I remember reading about a while ago.
- Around 50 million users use Amazon Prime. It makes sense that 50% of the users use this service.
- I would say the average purchase on Amazon is about $50 a month for active users. They pay nothing for shipping because of super saver shipping. That means we make $600 off each active user every year.
- A Prime user is most likely two times as likely to buy on Amazon, so we have $100 a month for a total of $1200 for each Prime user per year.
- I know Amazon has a low profit margin, so let's use a margin of 20%.
- Let's say the non-Prime customer purchases 12 times per year, whereas the Prime customer purchases 24 times per year.

Let's calculate the active user yearly profit:

$$Amazon\ Active\ User\ Yearly\ Profit$$
$$= \#\ Active\ Users * Purchases\ per\ Year * (Cost\ per\ Item * Profit\ Margin$$
$$- Super\ Saver\ Shipping)$$

$$Amazon\ Active\ User\ Yearly\ Profit = 50\ million * 12 * (\$50 * 0.2 - \$2)$$

$$Amazon\ Active\ User\ Yearly\ Profit = \$4.8\ billion$$

Let's calculate the Prime user yearly profit:

$$Amazon\ Prime\ User\ Yearly\ Profit$$
$$= \#\ Prime\ Users * Purchases\ per\ Year$$
$$* (Cost\ per\ Item * Profit\ Margin - Two\ Day\ Shipping) + Prime\ Annual\ Cost)$$

$$Amazon\ Prime\ User\ Yearly\ Profit = 50\ million * (24 * (\$50 * 0.2 - \$12) + \$99)$$

$$\textit{Amazon Prime User Yearly Profit} = \$2.55 \textit{ billion}$$

Hmm, I don't think I can reprice it and increase our profit. See, we want to avoid increasing the price, because that makes people unhappy, and even if we do we'll get less Prime users. If we decrease the price, we won't get that many Prime users anyway, and we'll decrease our profit.

INTERVIEWER: That's a bold statement. Why do you think decreasing the price won't get us more Prime users?

CANDIDATE: Amazon has done plenty of sales before. I don't think they were just sales. They were most likely testing the water to see if they can attract more users with a sale. The result hasn't been to their liking, which is why they've kept their $99 price tag.

One look through my formula and I can see why. I can plug in some numbers if you like to prove it.

INTERVIEWER: That won't be necessary.

Pricing Microsoft Azure

How would you price Microsoft's cloud service called Azure?

Things to Consider

- What are the strategic objectives? Maximize profits or share?
- Does pricing high, low or in-line with competitor's help Microsoft do so?
- What kind of creative pricing models can Microsoft invent?

Common Mistakes

- Not asking about costs.
- Not inquiring about Azure's unique value vs. the competition.
- Oversimplifying the situation by telling interviewer to just price below the competition.

Answer

CANDIDATE: This is a really complex problem. There are so many services to Azure. Are there certain services you want me to work with?

INTERVIEWER: That won't be necessary, just give me your thoughts on it.

CANDIDATE: Well, to be honest, I think what Azure is doing now is good. Because it has so many services, it's really easy to add and subtract modules and basically pay as you go. This goes for bandwidth or usage as well. If you use a lot of queries this month, for example, you just pay that much for it. If we try to slap a price on everything, it would get so complicated it would actually turn the users off.

INTERVIEWER: Well, do you think it can be improved in any way?

CANDIDATE: I supposed it could. We could offer bundle packages. For example, if you use service A and B but not C, we can offer a deal or bundle package that has A, B, and C. It would serve as a way to attract users to use C. But I think this will run the trouble of being too complicated for the user I mentioned above. I propose we actually offer monthly deals. We offer maybe one or two, and we gauge how users are reacting to them. For example, let say this month I am offering a deal for service A, B and C. I can gauge how many users made the switch to C, and how many stopped using C after the deal was over. That way it allows me to better price C.

We are doing this monthly because it's piecemeal. They only see one or two deals a month means they only need to decide on just two things. If it doesn't apply to them, they don't need to think about it. If we continue to test prices like this, we can eventually reach a good point on pricing for each service.

INTERVIEWER: That is an interesting thought. Why do you think Microsoft isn't doing this now?

CANDIDATE: Microsoft might be concerned with the confusion this brings, and also how customer service and business representatives would have to deal with extra inquiries. We might have some people whose deal ended but they don't know and they are complaining we are charging them more, and we might have people asking for deals on their particular service because they are used to seeing deals now.

Chapter 6 Analytics: Data Science

Weighing Eight Balls

You have eight balls all of the same size. 7 of them weigh the same, and one of them weighs slightly more. How can you find the ball that is heavier by using a balance and weighing it only twice?

Things to Consider

- Work out an example.
- Consider different edge cases.

Common Mistakes

- Assuming that it's a digital scale, not a balance.
- Solving for the best case with the balance, which is one weighing.
- Incorrectly assuming that the heavier ball can be determined without using the balance and simply identifying the heavier ball by hand.

Show your work below. Make any assumptions as necessary. Answer on the next page.

Answer

CANDIDATE: I would first weigh 3 vs. 3. We have two possibilities:

- The heavier ball is not in here. It's in one of the 2 balls I didn't weigh. I then weigh 1 vs. 1 on the remaining 2 balls to find it. I only weighed twice.
- The heavier ball is in one of the 3 balls. I then eliminate the other 5 balls. I then weigh 1 vs. 1 out of these 3 balls. The heavier ball is in either of these 2, in which case I would know, or the heavier ball is not, which then it must be the 3rd ball that I didn't weigh. I only weighed twice.

False Positives

Which is better? Having 10 false positives or 80 false positives?

Things to Consider

- If you're not clear on the definition, don't hesitate to ask the interviewer.
- If the interviewer doesn't respond to your clarification request, reason out the possible definition. Then confirm with the interviewer if you've arrived at the right definition.

Common Mistakes

- Pout when the interviewer won't define an unclear term for you.

Show your work below. Make any assumptions as necessary. Answer on the next page.

Answer

CANDIDATE: 80 false positives. This means we have a lot of room for improvement. Think about it, if I have an elaborate product and I am only seeing 10 false positives, there must be a lot of false positives we didn't discover yet. With 80, I feel a bit more confident. I am sure there are still some we didn't discover, but we found a lot this time.

INTERVIEWER: Wouldn't 10 false positives mean you have a more mature product?

CANDIDATE: It could, or it could mean our testing isn't as thorough. I rather be on the safe side.

Chapter 7 Product Design: Customer Journey Map Exercises

TurboTax Journey

Create the customer journey map for a Intuit TurboTax user.

Things to Consider

5Es Framework

Answer

Entice	Enter	Engage	Exit	Extend
• Uh oh, tax day is coming	• Get ready to purchase TurboTax • Investigate difference between TurboTax onlin vs. desktop • Purchase TurboTax desktop	• Enter personal information • Get confused about what to enter • Research issue online • Attempt to connect with Intuit customer service • Get answer and continue process • Reach out to company, bank and other 3rd party for supplemental information	• Submit tax return online or by mail	• Check for refund status, if applicable • Respond to additional inquiries from tax bureau, if applicable • Sign up for a reminder to purchase TurboTax for next year

Amazon Journey

Create the customer journey map for an Amazon customer.

Things to Consider

5Es Framework

Answer

Entice	Enter	Engage	Exit	Extend
• Research products	• Research options on Amazon or Google • Read reviews including Amazon and other sites found on the Internet • Establish a consideration set	• Select product to purchase • Compare prices • Investigate purchase policies including sales tax as well as shipping returns and fees	• Complete purchase • Check delivery status	• Return product • Contact customer service • Post product review

Chapter 8 Product Design: Pain Point Exercises

Facebook Pain Points

Rant about Facebook.

Answer

1. Feel guilty about wasting time on Facebook.
2. Get jealous of presumably amazing things others are doing.
3. Get in trouble, like losing a job, for posting sensitive information on Facebook.
4. Facebook messages must be viewed in a separate app on a mobile device.
5. Spam messages.
6. Ongoing changes with the newsfeed algorithm makes it difficult to see a chronological feed.
7. Privacy settings are confusing; people I don't know are viewing photos and other information intended for small audiences.
8. Too many ads.
9. Search is not useful in searching for friends' status messages.
10. Facebook is a superficial. It gives users the impressions that have a strong relationship between friends.
11. It's awkward to deny an acquaintance who wants to be my Facebook friend.

Crowdfunding Website Pain Points

Rant about the customer, not creator, experience with Kickstarter.

Answer

1. Unclear ship dates.
2. Late ship dates
3. Some products never ship at all.
4. Don't know who to invite.
5. Products are underwhelming.
6. There's no verification of a project's claims.
7. Popular pledge categories are limited and sold out already.
8. No or limited updates.
9. Don't like the peer pressure when friends ask to back a project.
10. Limited information about the creator.

Chapter 9 Product Design: Brainstorm Exercises

Netflix for Kids

Brainstorm at least 10 solutions to flag age inappropriate content for kids less than 10 years old.

Answer

Flag content based on:

1. Motion Picture Association of America (MPAA) ratings.
2. Known list of directors, with age inappropriate material.
3. Known list of actors, with age inappropriate material.
4. Known list of movie and TV studios, with age inappropriate material.
5. Content descriptions.
6. Visual recognition of inappropriate material, using human screeners.
7. Visual recognition of inappropriate material, using artificial intelligence.
8. Audio recognition of inappropriate language.
9. Text recognition of inappropriate language in transcripts.
10. Crowdsourced user reports.

Google Offline Search

Brainstorm at least 10 solutions to allow those who don't have Internet access to perform a Google search.

Answer

1. Store local Google index on user's computers for the most common queries such as weather, restaurants, etc. Refresh index when user connects to Internet café.
2. Allow access to a bigger Google index using a peer-to-peer networking technology, even without always-on Internet access.
3. Compress Google index onto a USB key; deliver a fresh USB key every morning a la newspaper delivery.
4. Deliver Google search results via automated voice call.
5. Deliver Google search results via manual voice call.
6. Deliver Google search results via text message.
7. Deliver Google search results via mail.
8. Deliver Google search results via courier.
9. Perform Google search via a publicly available Internet-connected kiosk.
10. Sponsor or subsidize Internet cafes, allowing users to perform Google searches.

Chapter 10 Product Design: Putting it Together

Amazon Mayday in Gmail

Let's say we wanted to implement an Amazon Mayday-like feature in Gmail. How would that work?

Things to Consider

- Distill the key features of Amazon Mayday and map the appropriate features to Gmail.
- Be prepared to defend design decisions including features left in and features left out.

Common Mistakes

- Making incorrect assumptions on how the feature works, especially for those who have never used it before.

Answer

CANDIDATE: Just so we are on the same page, Amazon Mayday is a feature that is on the Fire tablet that is essentially a panic button that lets you connect with a tech support for help. They can draw on your screen to show you where to go, do it for you, or give you instructions on how to do it.

INTERVIEWER: That is correct.

CANDIDATE: Okay. Can I get some time to brainstorm?

Candidate takes one minute.

CANDIDATE: Okay, I have a few ideas, but first let me point out some things. This needs to be displayed prominently somewhere on the Gmail page. It needs to be ever present no matter which page you are on. I would say somewhere in the top would be nice. Whenever the user hovers over it, it should display a description for what it is.

When the user presses it, it should automatically connect with a tech support. First though, it should detect which language you need it in. Since Gmail definitely tracks language, this makes it easier. The user then gets connected through Google Hangouts or Gmail (email thread). He then has three options:

- **Remote Desktop**. The customer service representative can remote desktop in to fix the problem. The user is warned that the customer service will be able to see his email, which may be sensitive.
- **Audio/Text**. The representative can use voice (if the user agrees and has a microphone and this is through Hangouts) or message the user through Hangouts or email. Instructions can be given this way for the user to follow.
- **Video**. Hangouts can do video calling or upload videos. The user can follow through that.

The biggest concern here is that the user must be the one that chooses which option to use. If we offer too many choices it could confuse the users, so we need to be selective. Looking back, I went into too much breadth. I would say we should only keep audio/text through Hangouts as the only option. This will also be easier to train customer service representatives.

At the end of the session, the user can rate the representative one to five stars; they can also write an optional one to line review. This will help us gauge how our representatives are doing and whether or not the users find this experience helpful.

INTERVIEWER: Why did you mention going through Gmail for help earlier instead of Hangouts?

CANDIDATE: I figured some people may not have Hangouts enabled or have never used it. If a window popped up randomly it might confuse some people. In hindsight, it's alright, because most programs like these do have a random popup on the side anyway.

INTERVIEWER: I like the fact that you mentioned privacy earlier. What if a user needs help but can't do it on his own even with audio help? He really wants the customer service to do it for him, but doesn't want to expose his sensitive email.

CANDIDATE: That could happen. Other than implementing some sort of thing to hide sensitive information (blur out all emails?) we can't really do it without the user's consent. That's a lot of work for the engineers though, so I wouldn't recommend it.

INTERVIEWER: But then the user would be really unhappy if the problem isn't resolved.

CANDIDATE: They would, and they'll blame Google for not helping with the problem. But, I still believe we should go with this solution. It's not perfect, but I think most people would give consent in this case, so I don't think engineers spending time to add this feature that most people won't use is worth it.

Changing Google Inbox

How would you change Google Inbox?

Things to Consider

- Who uses Google Inbox vs. the default Gmail interface?
- What are they trying to accomplish?
- What product improvements can Google Inbox make to better deliver on the brand promise?

Common Mistakes

- Spending too much time asking for context.

Answer

CANDIDATE: I would definitely start by unifying the inbox. Normally I'd approach this question by analyzing users and use cases then thinking of a few solutions. But this is something I've thought of for a long time.

Right now a lot of people have multiple email addresses. A typical user has an email for work and one for home. They would ideally want to have both available in one place. Gmail is in perfect position to take this market. Before the most popular aggregate mail client was Thunderbird, but it is no longer being supported. Outlook is a close competitor, but it doesn't actually do this unified inbox function well. New companies like Mailbird is rising up to the challenge and doing okay, so clearly there is a market for this.

A unified mailbox needs several functions:

- **Unified Inbox**. The user needs to receive emails from multiple accounts. These all need to be in one inbox.
- **Unified Sent Box**. The user needs to send emails as multiple accounts. The software adjusts based on which account received the email.
- **Multiple Mail Support.** This needs to support the most popular email providers like Yahoo, AOL, and Outlook / Hotmail. Less popular email providers can be supported under POP3 and IMAP.
- **Hangouts.** Users can log into Hangouts under multiple identities. If he has friend A on account X and friend B on account Y, he needs to talk to them as those accounts.

The reason why this is a great idea is because there is a clear need for this in the market. If a user is using something else like Mailbird, we cannot show ads to the user. With ads being the major source of revenue for Google as a whole, it's essentially we recapture this market.

INTERVIEWER: It's interesting you mentioned this. Why do you think Gmail has not thought of this yet?

CANDIDATE: I am sure they have, but they probably don't see a compelling reason to spend time on this. Companies like Mailbird hasn't exactly been blessed with skyrocketing users, and I am sure the majority of users don't have more than one email. However, it's a growing trend. I'm surprised big companies like Microsoft haven't invented similar products.

Disneyland and Google Products

Improve the Disneyland user experience, relevant to a Google product.

Things to Consider

- Use the CIRCLES method.
- Think of a big, moonshot idea.

Common Mistakes

- Not exploring the customer needs first.
- Not clarifying with the interviewer on whether it is about improving the general Disneyland experience or improving the Disneyland experience with Google products.

Answer

CANDIDATE: Can I get some time to brainstorm?

Candidate takes one minute.

CANDIDATE: I have a few ideas with Google Maps:

- **Estimated wait time and comments.** Showcase the estimated wait time for each attraction. People can also leave comments as ratings. Sample comments could be, "This attraction is great," "This one isn't that fun," and "This fun thing is over here!"
- **Directions for the place.** This one is simple. We simply have directions for the place. Disneyland can be huge and it would be easy to get lost. Sometimes, it's also hard to find where an attraction is, or say, the bathrooms or food.
- **Show times and important figures.** Showcase show times so people will know when to go. Also showcase where important figures will appear at when. There are a lot of costumed employees and it can be hard to track them down.

INTERVIEWER: Which one do you think will make the biggest impact?

CANDIDATE: Technically the latter two would be built on direction to the place, so that would be the biggest impact. Sometimes a lot of people get tired of trying to find something and leave. That's a frustrating experience. By showing them where everything is, they will spend more time enjoying and less time trying to figure out where they are. They will probably find exciting attractions they didn't know about and have a great time.

Grocery App

What features would you suggest for a grocery app?

Things to Consider

- Define customer segments; explore customer needs deeply.
- Give your feature ideas memorable names, so it is easier for your interviewer to record and recall.

Common Mistakes

- Unimpressive, commonplace ideas such as a grocery list app.
- Not drawing out wireframes to help the audience to visualize your solution.

Answer

CANDIDATE: Do you have a specific implementation in mind?

INTERVIEWER: No, you can design anything you want, as long as it has to do with groceries.

CANDIDATE: Can I get some time to brainstorm?

Candidate takes one minute.

CANDIDATE: I have a few users in mind when designing the app for groceries.

- **Bargain Hunters**. These are people who want to buy groceries on deal.
- **Cooking Enthusiasts**. These are people who likes cooking, but don't know a lot of recipes.
- **Health Conscious People**. These people may be people exercising or just people who want to get healthier.
- **The Undecided**. These people come in the grocery store not knowing what to buy because they have no idea what they want to eat next week.

I like buying stuff on deals, so I would like to focus on the Bargain Hunters persona.

INTERVIEWER: Okay.

CANDIDATE: I am thinking of three features:

- **Price Comparisons**. So for the Bargain Hunters, they can scan the bar code of the item they want to purchase and see price comparisons with nearby stores. This helps them save.
- **Coupon Finders**. Whenever they scan the code of an item, the bargain hunters can automatically download coupons (if applicable) for the item. They can also see coupons and weekly deals so they can decide what to buy.
- **Alternatives**. Whenever they scan an item, the app can give them cheaper alternatives (e.g., you can use chicken legs instead of chicken thighs in your stew because it's cheaper this week).

Out of all of these ideas, I think I like price comparisons more. It's a natural way to use your phone, and it's a very useful function. We can also track price points through this since we have data now. It also has a lot of advertising opportunities. The con is that scanning might take a lot of power, and it can be hard to hold a phone on one hand and your basket or kart on the other when shopping. It might also get tedious to scan every item you want to buy. On a typical trip to the grocery store, I would probably look at least 50-60 items.

Mobile App for Dentists

Design a mobile app for a chain of local dentist offices.

Things to Consider

- Product design discussions can be quite lengthy. Interviewers appreciate if you preview where the discussion is heading. E.g. "Let's imagine a typical visit first. It will help us understand gaps and how we want to improve it before thinking of solutions."

Common Mistakes

- Not connecting solutions with user problems.

Answer

CANDIDATE: Let's think about users first. I can think of two different users: patients and office staff. The office staff includes the receptionist, nurses and dentists.

Let's imagine a typical visit to the orthodontist office. This will help us understand gaps and how we want to improve the experience before thinking about solutions.

Patients want convenience. First, they browse for a local dentist. Then they'll look at reviews; it's also important that the dentist is covered by their insurance provider. Patients then call the dentist and provide insurance information. After that, patients describe their symptoms and discuss with the dentist. The patients schedule time to come in. The dentist's office sends reminders the day before the appointment.

Patients then comes in, show their insurance information and get dental work done. They pay and then leave. Sometimes patients make their next appointment, especially if it's a regular cleaning or multi-appointment procedure.

Based on the customer exploration, I notice a few things:

- Insurance gets involved a lot. It would be nice if this is automated.
- There is an inherent need for scheduling and reminders.
- Dentist can get helpful information in advance if patients can describe their symptoms using pictures or text. We can add a social element to this where other users can see and give the patient tips. The user might not even need a trip to the office.
- Payments may be a hassle; some offices might not take particular credit cards.

Now let's brainstorm features:

- **Insurance Info**. Users can upload his insurance information. When the patient tries to find a dentist, the app can show only dentists that accept his insurance.
- **Location Info**. Patients can look up dentists based on the patients' shared location. Furthermore, patients' location information can be shared 15 minutes before an appointment; the office can determine whether the patient will be on time or late.

- **Payment Info**. Users can store their payment information in the app. Users can pay through the app every time. The payment history feature will make it easier for the user to track their expenses.
- **Symptoms**. Patient can select what symptoms they have via pictures or text. When they contact a dentist, the dentist can peruse the users' selections and make a preliminary diagnosis.
- **Social**. Dentists and patients can talk to each other. Dentists can write blog articles with tips and tricks. Patients can ask questions about their symptoms and help each other out. Patients can also contact dentists and talk (e.g. what's wrong with my teeth, I am going to need to reschedule, I'll be late, etc.)
- **Scheduling**. Users can schedule through the app. Reminders will be sent automatically. This goes for scheduling an appointment as well as reminding users to come in for a biannual cleaning. The app should also store information about what days dentists will be available and available where (some dentists have multiple offices). This will save time, effort and frustration.

Attracting New Customers

Let's pretend you're trying to attract new customers to Amazon.com with the goal of turning them into recurring customers. What would you do to our website? How would you know if it's effective or not?

Things to Consider

- Despite the innocuous wording, this is a product design question, followed by a metrics question.
- Approach this question using the CIRCLES Method.
- Approach the metrics part of the question keeping AARM in mind.

Common Mistakes

- Not suggesting different hypotheses and explaining how they can be tested.
- Focusing on too many use cases.

Answer

CANDIDATE: Can I get some time to brainstorm?

Candidate takes one minute.

CANDIDATE: I can think of several ideas.

- **Show competitor pricing.** For every product, we'll show how much our competitors are selling them for. This is sort of like how Google Shopping is doing this. Because Amazon is going for low profit margin anyway, I feel like we won't have any problem with this. New users will see that Amazon has the cheapest price and come back to shop with us. If a certain product is indeed not the lowest price, we can also see from our data that we need to lower it because not enough people are converting. This would show as "Competitor Pricing" under our product page. We'll track all these links too and see which ones the users are going to.
- **We'll match your price.** This doesn't require any website changes at all other than a new policy page. Basically, if you buy a product, and you find a cheaper alternative within 7 days, we'll match your price by refunding you some Amazon credits. Customers feel safe in buying from Amazon because they'll always be guaranteed the best price. They'll also be refunded in Amazon credits, which means to use them they need to buy from us again.
- **Recurring coupons.** This is a newsletter change and not a website change. Basically every user would get a monthly coupon (e.g. flat 20% off). This reminds them to come back and shop at Amazon. For new users we can even give a big coupon upon sign up (e.g. 30% off). Most of the time the first conversion is the hardest, and then it's a lot easier for them to form a habit. By giving them a monthly coupon it incentivizes them to do so as well. We can even turn this into a system where you can track your progress and "win" your next coupon based on how much you've spent already.

Which one do you want me to focus on?

INTERVIEWER: I like the coupon idea. How would you know this is working?

CANDIDATE: Well, we can track a lot of data from the users right? For one, we don't have to just send it through the newsletter. We could be putting them in different websites. As long as we track them we can know where the new users saw this and converted. We can also track the number of monthly coupon usage as a whole, and see the adoption rate. This helps us to know how effective this is. We can then track our monthly purchases and see if they have gone up or not. If a recurring user, he'll definitely use our coupon. The question is, is he buying more as a result or still buying the same stuff?

Birthday Engagement

Birthdays are a popular event. How would you drive engagement on Facebook?

Things to Consider

- Clarify with the interviewer, if necessary. For instance, is the interviewer asking you to increase the number of:
    - Birthday event invitations via the Facebook platform
    - Birthday greetings on Facebook

Common Mistakes

- Suggesting marketing promotions and not product features.

Answer

CANDIDATE: When you say engagement, do you mean more engagement toward birthdays (meaning more people participating or hosting) or more engagement during birthdays (meaning more activities)?

INTERVIEWER: I mean more engagement toward birthdays. We want more people to host or join a birthday.

CANDIDATE: Oh, so this is more of a marketing problem.

INTERVIEWER: Well, it could be seen as one, but I want you to approach it from the product design point of view.

CANDIDATE: Can I get some time to brainstorm?

Candidate takes one minute.

CANDIDATE: I have a few ideas:

- **Best birthday party feature**. We host events on a monthly basis trying to feature the best birthdays. The community would vote on this. This is nice because it provides a really nice build up. Since birthdays are once a year, 11/12 people won't be able to host theirs. This gives them anticipation. Also they would join local ones (thus more engagement) to see what's up.
- **Biggest crowd contest**. The birthday that is the most common gets a prize for everyone who shares that birthday. This way people will try to host the biggest ones (increasing engagement) and people will try to be part of the biggest ones (increasing engagement).
- **Guess the birthday person's age**. Have the community vote. People who are the closest will get a chance to win something. The party that had the most wrong answers will win something as well. This way people will try to host birthday parties where the community have a really hard time telling the age. People will either want to test their luck or be part of one where they try to hide their age.

INTERVIEWER: Which idea would you recommend?

CANDIDATE: Best birthday contest is probably the easiest one to do. Biggest crowd contest is nice too but it would have a hard time tracking. Guess the birthday person's age seems attractive at the surface. However, it is not as all-encompassing as the best birthday contest; it could also draw unwanted attention or potentially bullying.

Microsoft in a Restaurant

How would you add any Microsoft product to a restaurant?

Things to Consider

- For newer restaurants, one of their biggest concerns is creating demand for their business.
- All restaurants are concerned with yield, table turnover, upsell and labor productivity. They also care about minimizing food and labor costs.

Common Mistakes

- Offering solutions without mentioning the restaurant's needs.
- Mentioning the restaurant's needs but not connection solutions to those needs.

Answer

CANDIDATE: Can I get some time to brainstorm?

Candidate takes one minute.

CANDIDATE: I am thinking of a few things:

- **Bing News**. Restaurants usually have a very long line, especially during lunch and dinner. I am thinking of having Bing News be available on a big screen TV while people are waiting for their food. This is good because it gives them something to do. It'll also promote Bing, and we can even show ads for specific restaurants. We can even do this while people are waiting for their food. I know this is a new concept in China where people can view ads, subscribe to an offer, and get a discount for the food.
- **Microsoft Azure**. Let say we are running a huge chain restaurant. Data tracking everything would be interesting. We can see what kind of menu items are popular depending on location, and we can see other things like paying habits (we can offer different prices based on location) and traffic flow. We can do this all through Azure and have it uploaded to a central database.
- **Bing Recommendations**. When people are sitting down to offer, they can use our Bing Recommendations to see what is good and what is not. We can even encourage users to rate, write reviews, and take pictures for a price off. This populates Bing Recommendations with data and introduces people to Bing.

I think I really like the Bing Recommendations idea.

INTERVIEWER: That is an interesting concept. What difficulty do you think we would face if we try to launch such a feature?

CANDIDATE: I am thinking we would need to have a really big business team. I know Microsoft has a very powerful business team that works with enterprises, but restaurants would be a new sector. Good thing we have experience, so applying that to another industry wouldn't be too hard. We would also need to work out individual price points with the restaurants to make sure it is a win-win situation for us. As long as we get users to use Microsoft products, not only are we promoting ourselves and increasing our branding, we are also getting opportunity to display ads for revenue.

INTERVIEWER: Wouldn't users be annoyed by being bombarded by ads when they are trying to enjoy their dinner?

CANDIDATE: We really need to approach this from another angle. Why do people think ads are intrusive? It's only bad when the ads aren't relevant to you. For example, while you are in line, you have nothing to do so seeing interesting news and ads is a good experience. While you are ordering food, ads to help you decide what to offer is a positive experience. While you are eating food, getting an ad for a price off is of value to the user. We can even promote things like local events (e.g. theaters, shows, clubs) to the user. If they are out for dinner, they are probably going to stay out after that too. This would be perfect as the ads are contextual.

Favorite Technology

What's your favorite technology and why?

Things to Consider

- Establish your criteria for your favorite technology.
- Explain the technology; don't assume the listener knows what you are talking about.
- Be clear, confident and detailed on why the technology meets your criteria.

Common Mistakes

- Failing to be specific about why it's your favorite.
- Choosing a stale, tired example like the Apple iPhone.
- Not comparing and contrasting with existing alternatives to help listener appreciate why your product is remarkable.

Answer

CANDIDATE: Can you give me a minute to brainstorm?

Candidate takes a minute.

CANDIDATE: The Microsoft Kinect is my favorite piece of technology because it satisfies my requirements. They are:

- How useful is it?
- How innovative is it?
- Is it easy to use and understand?

Screenshot / Microsoft

The Kinect is an Xbox attachment that can also be used on the PC as a motion capture device. It tracks your motion and can be used as an input for all sorts of applications, like games or software. It's immensely useful because it's a unique way for the user to control what's happening on screen.

It's also very innovative. It is the first of its kind for consumer use, which created a new consumer gaming genre. For example, dancing games are easier to play because you are actually dancing as opposed to tapping buttons on a controller.

The Kinect is also easy to use and understand. Turning it on, you see a silhouette of yourself on the top of the screen. Anything you do is reflected there. Depending on the game you are playing, the silhouette also follows your motion. The intuitive controls and instant feedback makes it so simple that even my grandma can use it.

To conclude, the Kinect is my favorite piece of technology because it satisfies my requirements for a good piece of technology: useful, innovative, and easy to use.

YouTube Tech Stack

What do you like about the YouTube tech stack?

Things to Consider

- Use the Rule of Three.
- It's very likely the next question to follow is, "What do you not like about the YouTube tech stack?"

Common Mistakes

- Clarify if you are not clear on what the interviewer means by "YouTube tech stack." The interviewer could be referring to YouTube's API or YouTube's technology in general.

Answer

CANDIDATE: Can I get some time to brainstorm?

Candidate takes one minute.

CANDIDATE: I can think of several ones I like:

- **Streaming.** YouTube has one of the best streaming technology in the world. Because YouTube serves billions of users per day, it's important every user is able to see the exact videos they want when they want without any hiccups.
- **Recommendation.** YouTube has billions of videos and new ones are being added at an alarming rate every second. It's important to showcase the most relevant videos to each user, and thus YouTube does this through its recommendation feature. It's a marvelous algorithm.
- **Server Load.** YouTube has more than 1.3 billion users. A small spike in users could be millions of users. YouTube must take all of this into account in its server architecture and network design.

INTERVIEWER: Which technology do you like the most?

CANDIDATE: Hmm, I think I like the server load the most. It's the most impressive. No other video has traffic like YouTube. Streaming is amazing, but it was really pioneered by a lot of other websites before. Recommendation is great, but it's not unique as sites like Netflix and Hulu has them too.

Airports in the Future

How do you envision the future of airports?

Things to Consider

- Treat vision questions about the future of X no differently than product questions. Use the CIRCLES Method.
- It may help to do the CIRCLES Method in the reverse order; that is, start with a big idea first and then work your way toward it.

Common Mistakes

- Not having a unique, compelling vision.
- Having a big vision, but not solving a big problem.
- Having a big vision that addresses an important problem, but failing to provide details around the technical implementation.

Answer

CANDIDATE: This is a very broad question. I think I would like to focus it down to several key ideas. Is that okay?

INTERVIEWER: Sure.

CANDIDATE: Let me get some time to brainstorm.

Candidate takes one minute.

CANDIDATE: I have a few ideas in mind. I am going to explain the key concept behind them and go from there.

- **Smooth Process.** Everything is bound by your smartphone, ID or whatever fancy device we all carry in the future. As soon as you walk in, your device tells you where to go. You won't be carrying any packages because those would have been pre-shipped to your plane and will be waiting for you when you arrive. You don't need passports or tickets because your identity has been confirmed through your device already. You don't need to go through security checks because of your identity. You simply show up 5 minutes before the plane starts sitting people, and walk through. No waiting and no hassles; it's a smooth process.
- **Uninterrupted Experience.** Whatever you were doing at home or at the airport will not be interrupted. Say you were watching a movie or reading a book. These content will be available for you at the airport or on the plane. Going to the airport and riding the plane will not interrupt your everyday life.
- **Preparation.** What you need, such as additional items or clothes or gifts, will be readied for you from the airport. This makes the airport journey that much smoother, because every preparation has been made for you.
- **Pleasant Waiting.** During flight transitions you could be stuck at an airport. The airport will be filled with activities you want to do, as well as comfortable places you can wait and rest in.

The key concept behind all of these is convenience. We want to make the airport situation pleasant. Right now, airports are a collection of people being confused, running late or waiting forever. Think about the different steps:

- Checking in your luggage
- Showing your passport
- Printing your tickets
- Waiting
- Getting in line
- Showing your tickets and identification, again

These are all things we don't need to do in the future thanks to better tracking technology. I've seen a glimpse of this technology when traveling by train in Asia; I imagine the technology can be adapted for air travel.

INTERVIEWER: What do you think are the biggest issues or challenges when trying to accomplish these ideas?

CANDIDATE: I think the biggest issue is privacy. It's a controversial topic right now and I am envisioning that we solved it in the future. I am not saying everyone will give up their privacy. That's a complicated topic. I am saying everyone will allow their interests and hobbies to be known for advertisement and convenience, kind like how the Internet works these days. We want to target ads and experiences most relevant to the user. It'll be a hard sell to some people, but I think we can achieve it in the future but it's also the biggest challenge to my idea.

Uses for Self-Driving Cars

What possible uses can you see for self-driving cars?

Things to Consider

- Creativity matters, so brainstorm as many ideas as possible.
- To facilitate brainstorming, prompts can be helpful. Consider the following types of prompts:
  - Personas: commuters, business travelers and vacationers.
  - Scenarios: disaster relief, warfare and humanitarian missions.
  - Vehicle type: sedan, sports car, convertible and sports utility vehicle (SUV).

Common Mistakes

- Forgetting about non-consumer applications
- Assuming that self-driving cars are unsafe
- Assuming that self-driving cars won't happen until the distant future

Answer

CANDIDATE: The big two branches of this would be consumer vs. business. With Google being a consumer-driven company, I think I would focus more on the consumer side of things.

INTERVIEWER: Okay.

CANDIDATE: I am thinking three scenarios:

- **Commuters**. This is a very obvious one. A lot of people would kill for self-driving cars during commutes. They can just work in the car and being stuck in traffic wouldn't even be that bad.
- **Disabled People**. A lot of disabled people (e.g. blind) cannot drive for obvious reasons. A self-driving car would solve this problem instantly.
- **Picking Up People**. This is more of a use case, since we would have so many users we can include this. I am thinking people who have had a few drinks or kids leaving school or soccer practice when their parents are not available. It would be very useful to have these people get home safely.

I do want to say that we might have trouble with the last two cases because I believe California just passed a law requiring the driver to keep at least one hand on the wheel for a self-driving car.

INTERVIEWER: It's interesting you mentioned that law. How do you see Google reacting to that?

CANDIDATE: I would think Google just needs more time to prove the safety of self-driving cars. People used to think airplanes were unsafe as well, but with time and enough adopters, it is now probably one of the most popular ways to travel. I think it's safer than boats or even trains.

Building a Product Review System

How would you build a product review system? What data would you use?

Things to Consider

- An MVC framework can help ensure your design is complete. That is:
    - What kind of inputs do you need? (Model)
    - What kind of outputs will be created? (View)
    - How would the inputs be manipulated to create the view? (Controller)

Common Mistakes

- Unstructured thinking and explanation that's hard to follow
- Missing critical pieces of the product review system such as detecting fraudulent reviews

Answer

CANDIDATE: Just to clarify, you mean the review system for goods being sold on Amazon, right?

INTERVIEWER: Yes. How would you build that one?

CANDIDATE: Do I have access to all data or am I limited?

INTERVIEWER: All data.

CANDIDATE: Alright, I'd recommend making our accuracy of reviews to be our main objective. Here is some data we should consider:

- Has the user actually purchased this product? If so, how long ago was that?
- Has this user actually changed or updated this review? A scenario I am thinking of is what if the user was happy for 3 months, then the product broke and he came and updated and changed his rating and review.
- Other users voting up or down on this review. Peer review is always nice.
- Has the user reviewed other products? Are those products related? What about the votes on those reviews?
- Did this user buy this product when it was a different price?
- Did the vendor contact the user? Was the problem resolved? Did the user bother to change his review?
- Has this user been on Amazon for long? I am thinking cases where people make new accounts and immediately rate down a product.

INTERVIEWER: There are some very specific cases in there. Do you think they are really necessary?

CANDIDATE: Yes. Selling on Amazon is a competitive market, and I can foresee some people trying to use underhanded tactics to sabotage their competitors. We need to net out false positives, otherwise our users will get a bad experience. That would be detrimental to Amazon.com.

INTERVIEWER: Which three do you feel are the most important factors?

CANDIDATE: Definitely these:

- Whether or not a user has purchased the product.
- Other users voting up or down on this review.
- Has the user reviewed similar products?

Bookshelf for Kids

Design a bookshelf for kids.

Things to Consider

- Use the CIRCLES design method.
- No need to mention or explore non-kid customer segments.
- When brainstorming is necessary, don't hesitate to pause. Quality thinking cannot occur by reacting.

Common Mistakes

- Superficially articulating the target customer.
- Not exploring customer needs deeply enough.
- Not coming up with a big, moonshot idea.

Answer

CANDIDATE: Can I ask for some clarifying questions?

INTERVIEWER: Sure.

CANDIDATE: Are we talking about kids in the United States or another country? Or are we talking about kids in general?

INTERVIEWER: Let's assume kids in the United States.

CANDIDATE: What age range are we talking about?

INTERVIEWER: Age 6 to 12.

CANDIDATE: Okay, so kids in elementary school. To reiterate, we are designing a bookshelf for kids from the age 6 to 12 in the United States. Is this correct?

INTERVIEWER: Yes.

CANDIDATE: Can I get a minute to brainstorm?

Candidate takes one minute.

CANDIDATE: I would like to first think about the users. We are making a bookshelf for kids, but the kids will not be the only user. Their parents or guardians would also be users, so we want to keep them in mind as well.

Now let me think of the regular bookshelf for adults. They have several problems for children.

Candidate writes the following on whiteboard.

- *Too tall*
- *Too heavy*

- *Too big.*
- *Unfit design*

The bookshelf can't be too tall, because otherwise the kids will have a hard time reaching for books. It can't be too short either, because adults need to use it. The bookshelf can't be too heavy either, because it would be a safety issue if it falls on the kid, and it won't need to be heavy because children's books are lightweight. Regular bookshelves are also too big, and since kids don't have that many books we don't need it that way. Even if kids to have lots of books, children's books are thin. As for the design, kids like bright colored stuff and they probably put stickers everywhere so wood and metal are not good materials.

I would also like to think of some use cases in case I missed anything by just thinking about the regular bookshelf.

The kids would do several things with it:

- Pull out a book. This will be a problem because children's books are really thin. If you pull out a book like this the rest of the row might collapse.
- Put in a book. Children's books are really thin, so it's hard to tell what book it is from the side.
- Move the shelf. Shelf can't be too heavy.

I think now I am ready to design features for this bookshelf.

INTERVIEWER: Okay, go ahead.

CANDIDATE: I have several features in mind.

Candidate writes the following on whiteboard.

- *Height is 4 feet.*
- *Width is about 2 to 3 feet.*
- *Made with plastic. Really lightweight.*
- *Comes in various bright colors.*
- *Comes with holders to help with books.*
- *Easy to add or remove sticky notes or stickers.*

The height is perfect for kids and still useable by adults. The width is not big but enough to hold children's books. It is made in plastic so it won't deform, but it's lightweight. Good for kids moving around and it is safe. It comes in bright colors so kids will love it. Also, I mentioned the problem with pulling out and putting in books before, and the holders should help with that. The plastic is also made to be easy to add or remove sticky notes or stickers. This will also help with the labeling problem, where books are too thin so it's hard to tell what it is.

Email for 7th Graders

Design an email system for a 7th grader.

Things to Consider

- Think broadly about the 7th grader's communication needs, especially since many might not use email today.
- No need to use all steps of the CIRCLES method, especially since the interviewer has made clear that he or she won't consider personas outside of 7th graders.
- Dive deep into the 7th grader's communication needs

Common Mistakes

- Arguing with the interviewer that a kindergartener would never use email.
- Suggesting a solution that feels like regular email and not tailoring it to the kindergartener persona.

Answer

CANDIDATE: Is this email system used in school only, or will there be no restriction to where they can use it?

INTERVIEWER: There is no such restriction.

CANDIDATE: Okay, I would like to first identify the users who will use this system. The kids are one, but their parents and teachers will definitely also be able to use it. At the least they will monitor them.

I would then think about the use case for this. What is the point of this system? Well, it's for 7th graders to connect with each other outside of school, mostly, but could also be used in school. They will be emailing their classmates, teachers and parents. You can send text, images, and videos. You can also attach things to the email.

With this in mind, I can think of a few features and restrictions:

- This email system must be an invite-only system. Meaning you need an administrator to add you to the system. This prevents unwanted people from entering.
- You cannot email anyone you don't know. You must be friends first. This is the second fail-safe in keeping unwanted people away.
- This system cannot receive emails from outside or send emails to the outside, with whitelisted emails being the exception. This way only teachers and parents can interact with this system.
- This email has strict filtering on, meaning everything is child-friendly.
- This email has IP restrictions. Children would only be able to log in at home and from school.
- Parents or teachers are mostly handling the login, since 7th graders probably have a hard time remembering their passwords. The admin can obviously reset passwords.

It has mostly similar features with existing emails. This one is more of a closed system within a school, but remember you can always become friends with people you want to email. So perhaps there is a "meet kindergarteners from Japan," and we can do it through this email if they too use a similar system. If not, we can just whitelist their emails.

The biggest concern is definitely safety. We don't want unwanted access, and we definitely want to keep it kid safe.

App for Celiac Patients

Design an app for a patient community affected by celiac disease.

Things to Consider

- Celiac patients have an adverse reaction to gluten-related food substances.
- Focus on how app technology can help patients live comfortably with the disease.

Common Mistakes

- Feeling uncomfortable with the interviewer is difficult and does not provide more context about what celiac disease is.

Answer

CANDIDATE: Just so we are on the same page, someone with celiac disease cannot have gluten-related food and other substances. If they do, it triggers a reaction in their small intestines which will lead to various symptoms like diarrhea, abdominal bloating and pain, and other side effects. In the long term, it may have serious health effects like vitamin or mineral deficiency.

INTERVIEWER: Yes, that is correct.

CANDIDATE: When you said app, I am assuming you want a mobile app?

INTERVIEWER: Yes.

CANDIDATE: Can I get some time to brainstorm?

Candidate takes one minute.

CANDIDATE: Okay, I have a few ideas:

- **Search Database**. People can look up, by text or speech, various food and items to see if they are safe to eat. They can also take a picture with their phone to ask the community. If possible, we would like image processing and auto-detect what kind of food this. Regardless, if something is not already in the database, the community can answer and add to the database.
- **Symptoms Lookup**. Same idea as the search database, except it is for symptoms. Type in or voice your symptoms; the app will see if it is a possible symptom for celiac disease in the database. If it is not, the community can offer advice on this particular symptom.
- **Restaurant Lookup**. Not all restaurants are gluten friendly. It would be helpful to find a directory of restaurants that are certified to accommodate gluten-free diets.

Sales and Inventory Tracking

Design a sales and inventory tracking system on the whiteboard.

Things to Consider

- Sales and inventory systems is used to track inventory and recording sales of a product.
- If a business carries more inventory than it can sell, the company not only spends money on warehousing costs, but their cash that was used to purchase inventory cannot be invested elsewhere in the business.
- One of the key components is to accurately forecast demand and purchase an optimal amount of inventory.

Common Mistakes

- Quitting on the problem after declaring that they're not familiar with sales and inventory tracking systems.
- Not wanting to draw on the whiteboard.
- Rushing through the solution, believing that the solution doesn't matter given the candidate's lack of familiarity with sales and inventory systems.

Answer

CANDIDATE: Let's think about what a sales and inventory tracking system needs. On a basic level, you should be able to add quotes and orders. Most of the screen is taken up by viewing a specific order.

Orders should have a company, contact, phone number, order date as well as shipping and billing address. We will also need order status: paid, processing, invoiced, canceled, etc. It should also have a breakdown of the order and price. For example, you ordered 4 X and 2 Y, they each cost this and the subtotal is that.

Let me draw the user interface.

Candidate draws the following on the board.

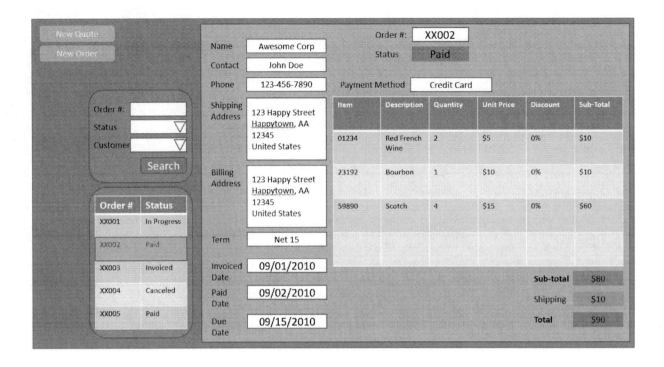

New Quote

New Order

Order #: [   ]

Status [▽]

Customer [▽]

[Search]

Order #	Status
XX001	In Progress
XX002	Paid
XX003	Invoiced
XX004	Canceled
XX005	Paid

Name [Awesome Corp]

Contact [John Doe]

Phone [123-456-7890]

Shipping Address
[123 Happy Street Happytown, AA 12345 United States]

Billing Address
[123 Happy Street Happytown, AA 12345 United States]

Term [Net 15]

Invoiced Date [09/01/2010]

Paid Date [09/02/2010]

Due Date [09/15/2010]

Order #: [XX002]

Status [Paid]

Payment Method [Credit Card]

Item	Description	Quantity	Unit Price	Discount	Sub-Total
01234	Red French Wine	2	$5	0%	$10
23192	Bourbon	1	$10	0%	$10
59890	Scotch	4	$15	0%	$60

Sub-total [$80]

Shipping [$10]

Total [$90]

Elevators in a Building

Design an elevator system for the following building:

- 100 floors in the building
- 3 total occupants
    - Occupant 1 is a company that occupies the top 10 floors.
    - Occupant 2 is a company that occupies 45 floors below occupant 1.
    - Occupant 3 is a company that occupies 45 floors below occupant 2.

Things to Consider

- Interviewer is looking for a logical and thoughtful elevator allocation.
- Clarify assumptions upfront such as population, peak hours and average load.

Common Mistakes

- Forgetting that some elevators should be reserved for maintenance teams or emergency responders.

Answer

CANDIDATE: I'm guessing you want the overall percentage allocation, not the actual number of elevators for the building right?

INTERVIEWER: That's correct.

CANDIDATE: Do you have information about the number of people on each floor?

INTERVIEWER: Assume that every floor has the same number of occupants.

CANDIDATE: Should I worry that the elevators are too small or won't function properly if it's too heavy?

INTERVIEWER: Let's say that the size of the elevator and the acceptable weight load is not part of this problem.

CANDIDATE: What are the peak hours of usage?

INTERVIEWER: Since we're short on time, let's not worry about the peak hours of usage. Can you wrap your answer in the next two to three minutes?

CANDIDATE: Sure, give me a moment to digest the information I know so far, and I'll be prepared to give you your recommendation.

Candidate takes one minute.

The obvious thing to do is allocate 10% of the elevators to occupant 1 and then 45% each to occupants 2 and 3. However, this assumes that that current occupant configuration will stay fixed. We cannot assume this. Corporate tenants come and go.

Instead, I would preserve flexibility for the building owner so that he can accommodate different tenant configurations. Thus, I would balance the elevators across the 100 floor building into rough thirds. That is,

- Elevator bank #1 would serve floors 1-33
- Elevator bank #2 would serve floors 34-66
- Elevator bank #3 would serve floors 67-100

I would also dedicate a special bank of three to four maintenance elevators which can also be used for emergency responders.

We can also allocate more elevators to elevator banks two and three, adjusting for the fact that they have to travel farther than elevator bank #1. Also, the lower floors may be served by a stairwell or an escalator system.

INTERVIEWER: Let's hear some numbers. How would you distribute these?

CANDIDATE: Should I give you a ballpark figure or actual numbers?

INTERVIEWER: Ballpark is fine.

CANDIDATE: Here's my breakdown:

- Maintenance elevators: 5% of overall elevator pool
- Elevator bank #1: 25% of overall
- Elevator bank #2: 30% of overall
- Elevator bank #3: 40% of overall

INTERVIEWER: Thank you.

Volume Up, Volume Down

Let's say you have a TV remote with 3 buttons, mute, volume up and volume down. What would you expect to happen if a user hits volume up button when its muted? Talk through the scenarios and what the user is trying to do. What would you expect to happen if you hit volume down button when it's muted?

Things to Consider

- The interviewer is trying to understand your ability to understand and justify design choices.
- It's also testing a candidate's design empathy. That is, can the individual deduce what the function the designer has intended?

Common Mistakes

- Not illustrating the different scenarios.
- Not clarifying the user's intent or the mental model.
- Not clearly explaining why an alternative design choice is inferior to the one they've chosen.

Answer

CANDIDATE: Is this one of those TVs where the mute button causes it to mute but keeps the volume or where mute actually makes the volume become 0. I've seen both types of TV.

INTERVIEWER: That's interesting. I've never encountered TVs that has the mute go to 0 when mute is hit. Let's try the latter TV types.

CANDIDATE: For volume up, I would say it's really three scenarios:

1. **User doesn't know the TV is muted**. The user thought maybe the volume is too quiet, and he wants to raise it.
2. **User does know the TV is muted**. The user does know the volume is muted, but he wants to hear it now and is too lazy to press the mute button again.
3. **User pressed it by accident**. In this case the user probably wants to unmute it, because there are only 3 buttons on the remote. What else can he do?

In this case, assuming volume 10 is very quiet and volume 100 would be the loudest setting, I would say whenever the user presses volume up, it should unmute and go automatically to volume 10. It would then very slowly increase the volume (slower than usual). After 5 seconds, a key press should increase volume at a regular rate. Below 10 is practically silent on most TVs, and doing this will make it easier for the user to increase the volume. We make it slower in the beginning so the user has time to react (let go of the button or drop the volume down because they only want 5 or something).

For volume down, I would say it's the same three scenarios again:

1. **User doesn't know the TV is muted**. The user wants to know if the current scene is silent or is the volume actually muted.
2. **User does know the TV is muted**. The user does know the volume is muted, but he wants to hear it now at a quiet volume and is too lazy to press the mute button again.
3. **User pressed it by accident**. In this case the user probably wants to unmute it, because there are only 3 buttons on the remote. What else can he do?

I'll assume volume 10 is very quiet again. I would say whenever the user presses volume down, it should unmute and go automatically to 10 like above. It would then very slowly decrease the volume (faster than usual). After about 5 seconds it should decrease it at a regular rate. It's for the same reason as above. We make it faster in the beginning because it's better to be softer than louder. Louder might make other people upset. Softer just might annoy the user for a few seconds but it won't be that big of a deal compared to it being louder than expected.

Design a Teleporter

Design a teleporter. What features would it have?

Things to Consider

- Use the CIRCLES Method.
- Explore customer needs deeply.

Common Mistakes

- Not clarifying the target persona.
- Not connecting the solutions with a specific target customer or use case.

Answer

CANDIDATE: It depends on the constraints and features of the teleporters itself. Could I ask some clarifying questions for them?

INTERVIEWER: Sure.

CANDIDATE: Who is using this teleporter? Regular people? Military?

INTERVIEWER: Regular people.

CANDIDATE: Can this teleport transport life? Or can it just transport inanimate objects?

INTERVIEWER: It can teleport life.

CANDIDATE: Is the cost pretty low? It feels like it has to be if it is serving regular people.

INTERVIEWER: Yes, it's nearly free.

CANDIDATE: Is this the cost for the teleportation or the teleporter?

INTERVIEWER: The act of teleportation is nearly free. The teleporter itself is still pretty expensive.

CANDIDATE: Does teleportation get more expensive with distance, weight or number of objects? How expensive?

INTERVIEWER: Let's just say it's impractical outside of local uses, and you can't really transport more than one person at a time.

CANDIDATE: Alright, I think I get the whole picture. Can I get some time to brainstorm?

Candidate takes one minute.

CANDIDATE: I have a few features in mind:

- **Powering up signal & percentages.** I am assuming the teleporter has a cool down period. It needs to be able to display this with light up effects and/or percentages so it's clear to everybody what's going on.
- **Screen doors.** Going to need screen doors to both protect people from trying to enter a teleportation in progress (and causing problems because you can't transport more than one person at a time), and let people see what's going on so they don't get shocked.
- **Waiting room.** We need a waiting room for people to wait in. Ideally this is used for commuting and there will be a lot of people.
- **Camera feed.** Camera feed of all the different destinations. People need to know other people got out fine.
- **Multiple teleporters.** We are going to need multiple ones in one so we can service people faster. Otherwise it's not really useful.
- **Automatic ticketing.** This will help, because I am imagining even people who drive to work would want to use our teleporter.

INTERVIEWER: Which feature would you say is the most important?

CANDIDATE: Probably the screen doors. Safety is top priority. If something bad happens people are never going to trust our machines again.

INTERVIEWER: Which feature do you think will take the longest or most cost to include?

CANDIDATE: I would imagine the waiting room. Ideally we want to have hubs of these around to get around the distance problem, and we want to all have it in one place. It'll actually take a lot of space because the waiting rooms will take up most of it. Real estate is expensive.

Innovative Refrigerator

Design an innovative new refrigerator.

Things to Consider

- Use the CIRCLES design framework.

Common Mistakes

- Not going into the implementation details. E.g. "The refrigerator will magically tell you when to reorder milk when it's out."
- Not picking a single use case to focus on. For example, some candidates attempt to tackle multiple things in the interview question – figuring out what to cook, how to store and food and how to replenish food. Doing so sacrifices the answer quality.
- Not being bold or aggressive enough is suggesting a unique and creative idea.

Answer

CANDIDATE: Is there a specific user group you have in mind?

INTERVIEWER: Just regular people.

CANDIDATE: What about pricing? Does that limit us?

INTERVIEWER: Yeah, about the same price as the standard refrigerator.

CANDIDATE: Okay, just to iterate, we are designing an innovative new refrigerator meant for middle class / regular people, and around the same price as common refrigerators.

INTERVIEWER: That is correct.

CANDIDATE: Okay, can I get some time to brainstorm?

Candidate takes one minute.

CANDIDATE: Okay, I got a few ideas in mind. First I want to talk about how I came to these ideas. I thought of common problems with your regular refrigerators and I want to solve these. Here are the common problems:

- There is not enough space in a regular refrigerator. There is a lot of wasted space between the door and the innards.
- The needs of whether you need the regular space vs. the freezer are different for different people.
- The shelves are never going to satisfy most people. Depending on how many people are using them and people using them, sometimes a shelf space would be too big and another would be too small.

Across these three pain points, the common theme is: storage. So I will brainstorm some ideas on how to make refrigerators better at storing food:

- **Extra Middle Layer**. Basically add a layer between the door and the innards. By pressing a button on the handle, you can switch the middle layer to be on the innards (meaning it covers the insides) or on the door. Now you essentially have 3 layers you can access.
- **Movable Ceiling**. The ceiling separates the freezer and the rest of the fridge. We want to make it movable so the user can decide how much space they want for each. Obviously there are limits to how much you can move it, but it'll be better than the current fridges.
- **Modular Compartments**. This addresses the shelf problem. By adding slots on the side and allowing you to remove the floor to each shelf, you can decide how big shelves are depending on your needs.

I've tried to go for simple and cheap solutions to everything. Since we are limited by budget we don't want any fancy or high tech solutions that would incur a bigger cost.

INTERVIEWER: Do you have an estimation of how much extra this will cost?

CANDIDATE: Off the top of my head, it probably won't cost that much extra. Maybe around 10-15%. A lot of these are just redesigns. We are still using the same materials. I can get a more specific number if you want me to do the calculations.

INTERVIEWER: That's all the time we have.

Replacement for Set-top box

Design a replacement for the set-top box in a hotel room.

Things to Consider

- Contemplate the key functions of a set-top box.
- Consider the flaws by comparing against the competition, substitutes or workarounds.

Common Mistakes

- Wasting time by asking irrelevant questions.
- Not coming up with big, moonshot-caliber ideas.

Answer

CANDIDATE: Are we limited by cost or anything else?

INTERVIEWER: Yes, this cannot cost more than a set-top box.

CANDIDATE: How much does a set-top box cost in average?

INTERVIEWER: Around $250.

CANDIDATE: Okay. Let me first sum up what a set-top box does so we can see if we can think of alternatives to provide the same functions.

- **Play videos from various sources**. This includes cable and other channels. A big channel selection makes it more attractive.
- **On-demand videos**. You can play some movies and TV shows on demand.
- **Record videos**. You can record and schedule your favorite shows at any time.
- **Parental controls**. Perfect for those with kids.
- **Favorite channels**. With so many channels, this feature comes in handy. This is probably something we want to wipe or reset back to a few default channels each time we get a new guest.
- **Buttons on the device**. You can use buttons on the box itself in case your remote is missing or out of battery.

Now let us think of alternatives. This is in a hotel room, so we need to make sure there is no personal information when we pick alternatives. This means accounts are probably not a good idea. We should just have the hotel be able to set what kind of shows are available and have it reset when the guest leaves.

Let me get some time to brainstorm.

Candidate takes one minute.

CANDIDATE: I have a few ideas:

- **Smart TV**. This is the most obvious alternative. We can adapt popular consumer examples, such as Chromecast and Apple TV, to an enterprise setting. The hotel can request 50-100 accounts and assign each to each room. The content is restricted and handpicked by the hotel; parental controls can also be added.
- **Customized PC**. We can have a PC that is locked to only be able to view YouTube, Netflix and Hulu. Like the Smart TV, we can have content that is restricted and handpicked, and parental control.
- **TV**. Not your average TV, but the ones with a lot of features in them. These days, a lot of services like cable will offer similar features like a set-top box.

Both of these wouldn't cost very much. The Smart TV can be as low as $50, and probably cheaper in bulk. The PC doesn't need anything that requires amazing hardware, and in bulk it would be cheaper. The TVs should be ok in terms of price since it's just subsidized as part of the cost of the TV.

INTERVIEWER: Which one would you recommend?

CANDIDATE: I am going to rule out a customized PC. It is an extra device which can make the hotel room feel cluttered; it is also redundant. Most travelers carry their own devices such as smartphones, laptops and tablets that are capable of viewing content from YouTube, Netflix and Hulu. The TV option would require a mass hardware upgrade that can be costly. The Smart TV option is my favorite because it allows hotels to enhance existing TVs with new features using a relatively inexpensive Chromecast or Apple TV-like device.

Design a Thermos

Design a thermos.

Things to Consider

- Use the CIRCLES method.
- Interviewer may have intentionally left the prompt ambiguous. I would recommend that you treat this as "how would you design a better thermos" not "how would you make a regular thermos." If there's confusion, clarify with the interviewer.

Common Mistakes

- Uninspired suggestions such as keeping liquids warmer for longer periods of time, without specifying how this will be achieved or explaining the technology that goes into it.

Answer

CANDIDATE: Who will be using this thermos?

INTERVIEWER: This is designed mostly for patients. Their relatives will be using this to store food for them.

CANDIDATE: Are there any restrictions I should keep in mind? Such as cost.

INTERVIEWER: This should cost no more than $50 as the final price.

CANDIDATE: Alright. So just to make sure we are on the same page, we are making a thermos used mostly for patients for storing food. It should cost no more than $50.

INTERVIEWER: That is correct.

CANDIDATE: So we really have three groups of users: patients, their relatives, and hospital employees.

The use cases are simple. We are storing food, taking out food, standing still and keeping food warm or cool.

Since we are talking about patients here, it's most likely to keep food warm. It's also most likely for soup or congee.

There are a few features and restrictions we must keep in mind:

- This must be very tightly bound so the smell doesn't escape it. We also don't want germs to enter.
- This must not make a lot of sound, even when dropped. Hospitals should be quiet.
- This must look anything but white, because hospitals are mostly white and we want this to stand out.
- This should be able to store and take out soup easily.
- It should be able to store at least 3-4 portions.
- It should be lightweight with a good grip. Patients may have trouble using it otherwise, since they'll be weaker.
- It must be easy to clean and disinfect.

- Have a place to write names. There are a lot of patients in the hospitals and it could be confusing. The last thing we want patients to mix up this type of stuff which can transfer germs and diseases.
  The materials must be durable yet inexpensive. Patients might accidentally knock it on the ground. We are also restricted by price.

Design a Windshield Wiper

Innovate a new windshield wiper design.

Things to Consider

- Windshield wipers is not something most of us think about often. Take a moment to understand the purpose and pain points of a windshield wiper before proceeding.
- Decrease your probability of suggesting mediocre solutions by deeply exploring pain points.

Common Mistakes

- Suggesting a final recommendation that a combination of all your brainstorm ideas.
- Better candidates focus on brainstorm solutions for a single problem. It increases the chances of getting an impressive solution. Similarly, there's not enough time to come up with impressive solutions when there's more than one problem to tackle.

Answer

CANDIDATE: Is this a windshield wiper on a regular car or truck or something else altogether?

INTERVIEWER: This is a windshield wiper on a regular car.

CANDIDATE: Is there a cost restriction?

INTERVIEWER: Yes, it shouldn't cost over $50. Regular windshield wipers cost around $10.

CANDIDATE: Let me list out some problems with regular windshield wipers:

- Doesn't wipe the whole windshield.
- Hard time cleaning things like bird poop.
- Doesn't clean 100%.
- During heavy rain, it's not enough.
- Definitely can't power through snow.
- Can't clear ice on windshield.

I have some ideas to address these problems:

- The windshield wiper needs to be redesigned in a way to be able to wipe most, if not all of the windshield. Not being able to wipe the whole thing is not a big deal at first until you realize all the dirt and things get stuck on your windshield because that's as far as the wiper goes.
- It needs to have two separate modes. One for regular stuff (light dirt, rain) and one for heavy stuff (bird poop). The blade needs to be designed a bit differently for the heavy mode.
- It should have two things it can dispense, water and soap. This needs to be hooked up to the car.
- Remember the wiper has two functions: clean and prevent rain and snow. For the rain, during heavy rain it really isn't enough. It needs a smarter design. Maybe it can go up to the top of the windshield and cover it, causing rain to drip over to the side of the car.

- For heavy snow, it can't move away snow that has settled in during the night. It needs to be able to lift heavier things so it can clear piled up snow.
- To de-ice, the windshield wiper needs to be able to dispense vinegar. That helps de-icing.

Now that I think about it, the snow and ice features should only be available to the "North Edition." The regular edition does not need these. These two editions should be sold separately and priced separately.

Improving Toothpaste

How would you improve toothpaste?

Things to Consider

- Pick a specific persona.
- Explore customer needs.
- Use Rule of Three.

Common Mistakes

- Afraid of suggesting inferior ideas.
- Spending too much time asking for context.
- Not using vivid details, such as dental plaque, halitosis, gingivitis, fluoride and sodium bicarbonate. It makes the answer more credible, engaging and memorable.

Answer

CANDIDATE: There's many personas I can consider, but unless you disagree, I'm going to focus on the persona I know best: myself.

INTERVIEWER: Sure, that's fine.

CANDIDATE: There are many reasons why I brush my teeth including:

1. Health reasons
2. Need for fresh breath
3. Social norms

Here are some problems specifically with toothpaste:

1. I am afraid it is made of harmful chemicals as well as artificial sweeteners or colors.
2. I never know how much toothpaste is enough.
3. It's always hard to get the last bit of toothpaste.
4. I don't feel like they freshen my breath.
5. Some toothpastes are way too strong. If you get them on your tongue, it's very uncomfortable.

Now I can better think of ways to improve them.

1. Make it freshen your breath longer or stronger. This might be mutually exclusive with the next one.
2. Make the toothpaste tamer.
3. Make it a controlled or measured squeeze. That is, give an audible noise or click when the user has squeezed enough. Alternatively, build a one-click mechanism that determines the amount for each user. Most of us over squeeze toothpaste anyway.
4. Create a toothpaste that is free of chemicals such as sodium lauryl sulfate, which is a known pesticide.

I say let's focus on #3. #4 is a real concern, but I see plenty of Burt Bees' type companies offering organic toothpaste. #1 and #2 is interesting, but I'd say focus on #3. We have an opportunity to have a unique solution in the marketplace that solves a big problem.

Chapter 11 Metrics: Brainstorming Exercises

Tinder Metrics

What top metrics would you track for the Tinder online dating app?

Answer

Acquisition

- Downloads

Activation

- Active Users
- Visits

Retention

- Time in app
- Ratings
- Churn

Monetization

- In-app revenue
- Customer lifetime value

Amazon Seller Marketplace Metrics

What top metrics would you track for the Amazon Seller Marketplace?

Answer

Acquisition & Activation

- \# of Amazon customers with at least one click on the third-party marketplace page

Retention

- Average clicks on third-party marketplace page per Amazon customer
- CTR for third-party marketplace listings
- % satisfied transactions
- Net promoter score

Monetization

- Revenue
- Avg. transaction size
- \# of transactions

Other

- \# of buyer satisfaction claims: order not received, product not as indicated

Seller side

Acquisition

- Sellers
- Seller growth rate

Activation

- Sellers with at least 1 listing

Retention

- Gross marketplace volume
- Seller feedback ratings

Monetization

- Gross marketplace volume
- Buyer messages per transaction
- Conversion rate

Other

- # of sellers with buyer satisfaction claims

Chapter 12 Metrics: Prioritization Exercises

Bēhance Metrics

Imagine you are the product manager for Bēhance, a social network where designers can display and discover creative work. What's the most important metric for your product?

Things to Consider

- AARM framework
- Popular metrics for user-generated content sites, featured in *PM Interview Questions*

Common Mistakes

- Forgetting about timeframe for a particular metric
- Choosing a lagging metric such as Bēhance likes vs. a leading metric such as projects uploaded

Answer

CANDIDATE: Let me start by brainstorming potential metrics:

- Acquisition
    - Visitors
    - Returning visitors
- Activation
    - Registered users
- Retention
    - Views
    - Likes
    - Comments
    - Projects uploaded
    - Adds to a collection
    - Users with at least 1 project uploaded , all-time
    - Users with at least 1 project uploaded, in the last 30 days
- Monetization
    - N/A

Bēhance users are looking for visual inspiration. Users won't feel inspired if projects aren't fresh and new. Therefore, I would say the most important metric is the growth in new projects. That metric will drive growth for downstream metrics including:

- Visitors
- Returning visitors
- Views
- Likes

- Adds to a collection
- And possibly even new registrations

Prioritize Sales Metrics

The sales team's goal is to achieve $5M in new revenue each quarter. What's the one metric we should focus on?

Things to Consider

- What are the sales drivers? Hint: Outlining the sales funnel will help.
- Which goals are measurable, actionable and relevant to end goal?

Common Mistakes

- Choosing a metric without justification
- Not brainstorming a list of potential metrics first

Answer

CANDIDATE: Let me start by brainstorming potential metrics by looking at the sales funnel:

This is not going to be an easy call. All five metrics affect total revenue. Can you provide more insight on how the sales department is performing relative to these metrics?

INTERVIEWER: Go ahead and make your own assumptions.

CANDIDATE: For the sake of time, I'll make two assumptions. First, I'll assume our quarterly revenue is $4M. Second, I'll assume that average deal value is $10K.

INTERVIEWER: Works for me.

CANDIDATE: Based on my experience, I'll recommend that we focus on average deal value as our most important metric and target an increase from $10K to $12.5K. Here's why:

- **Customer Trust**. It's easier to get wins at the end of the sales funnel vs. the beginning. We've established customer trust; we're also a lot closer to securing purchase commitments. It's a lot easier to sell additional products or services at that stage of the sales pipeline. We can also consider increasing contract terms.

- **Measurable**. Deal size is very easy to measure and track. It's logged into most contract systems. Lead tracking in the earlier part of the funnel is notoriously error prone, especially if a busy salesperson forgets to input a lead.
- **Relevant**. Increasing deal size will make a clear impact on the $5M quarterly goal.
- **Actionable**. It's likely our team already have or can easily get training, scripts and sales materials to more effectively increase average deal size.

INTERVIEWER: Why didn't you choose closed deals?

CANDIDATE: Getting more closed deals isn't a trivial process, unless there's a bounty of qualified leads that are near closing stage. If our sales pipeline is thin, then getting more closed deals would require filling the funnel with more leads. Lead generation is not easy. Identifying new leads, contact them, developing a relationship and closing deal – not only is that a lot of work but also takes time. It may be years before we get tangible results.

INTERVIEWER: Thank you.

Chapter 13 Metrics: Diagnose Exercises

Diagnose Bēhance Metrics

As the Bēhance PM, let's say the number of original projects uploaded is down 5% week over week. Diagnose what happened.

Things to Consider

- List out all the factors that affect number of original projects uploaded.
- Evaluate each one.

Common Mistakes

- Missing a critical driver such as number of new projects completed. Or percent of completed projects that have been uploaded vs. not.

Answer

CANDIDATE: Let's first consider all the possible reasons why Projects Uploaded might be down.

Candidate writes the following on the whiteboard.

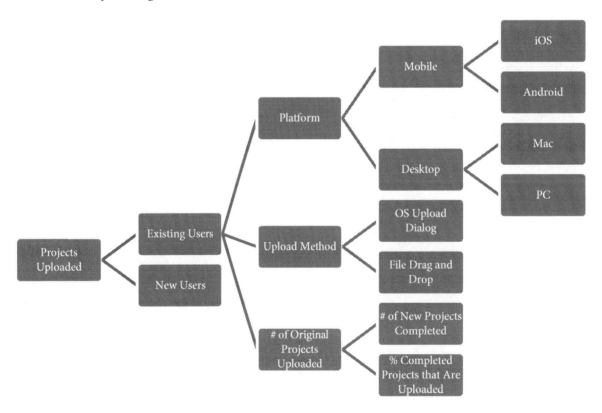

INTERVIEWER: That's an impressive list.

CANDIDATE: Thank you.

INTERVIEWER: So how would you isolate down the problem?

CANDIDATE: So new projects uploaded can come from existing or new users. Is there an issue with new users?

INTERVIEWER: Let's assume that there's nothing going on with new users.

CANDIDATE: Let's explore the existing user branch. The three things that can affect new projects uploaded from existing users can include:

- # of Original projects uploaded
- Upload method
- Platform

Did I miss any?

INTERVIEWER: That looks like a good list.

CANDIDATE: Let's start from the bottom first. Is there anything that indicate changes in the following:

- Number of new projects completed
- % completed projects that are uploaded

INTERIEWER: What do you think would affect the number of new projects completed?

CANDIDATE: Seasonality. Number of new projects completed are usually down on weekends and holiday seasons like summer.

INTERVIEWER: Good intuition, but let's say there's nothing in our research that indicate that's the issue.

CANDIDATE: Okay, let's go to the top of the list. Do we have data that indicates pins are down by device – whether it's mobile or desktop?

INTERVIEWER: Weekly visits on those devices seem to be normal, but the number of new projects uploaded is down on PC and Mac.

CANDIDATE: There could be three reasons for it: OS upload dialog and drag-and-drop

INTERVIEWER: You got it. Uploads via drag-and-drop is down on both PC and Mac.

CANDIDATE: What happened?

INTERVIEWER: Nice job answering the question. We pushed out a new server-side change last week that crippled drag-and-drop upload. We just resolved the issue yesterday with a new server-side release.

Diagnose Sales Metrics

We, the sales team, missed the $5M in new revenue target last quarter. Diagnose what happened.

Things to Consider

- List out all the factors that can affect new revenue.
- Evaluate each one.

Common Mistakes

- Wasting time exploring existing revenue, given that the question prompt is about new revenue.

Answer

CANDIDATE: If we missed the $5M new revenue target, that must mean:

1. We closed fewer deals than expected.
2. We closed deals at a lower average deal size.
3. Both 1 and 2 happened.

INTERVIEWER: Average deal size was not bad. In fact, it was 5% higher than expected.

CANDIDATE: Then it must be the number of closed deals.

INTERVIEWER: Correct.

CANDIDATE: Let me brainstorm reasons why number of closed deals may have gone done last quarter. I'll start by drawing out the sales funnel:

Working backwards from closed sales, did we have issues convert sales qualified leads into closed sales?

INTERVIEWER: No, the conversion rate from sales qualified leads to closed sales was well within our expectation.

CANDIDATE: How about the conversion rate from marketing to sales qualified leads?

INTERVIEWER: That conversion ratio was within our expectation as well.

CANDIDATE: How about the conversion rate from unqualified to marketing?

INTERVIEWER: The conversion rate was down, but it doesn't explain the whole story.

CANDIDATE: Let's start with the reduced conversion rate from unqualified to marketing qualified leads. Are there any hypothesis there?

INTERVIEWER: What do you think the reasons might be?

CANDIDATE: Thinking off the top of my head, here are some reasons why marketing qualified leads went down:

- Marketing vendor did not follow up on qualified leads
- Lead quality went down, making it harder to qualify

INTERVIEWER: Why do you think lead quality might go down?

CANDIDATE: Lead quality can go down when:

1. Can't find enough high-quality prospects
2. Can find high-quality prospects, but don't have the right contact information
3. Leads may have purchased in a more favorable economic environment but not now

INTERVIEWER: Okay, these are all good ideas.

CANDIDATE: So what actually happened?

INTERVIEWER: We had a re-organization where we hired a new VP of marketing. The new VP of marketing froze our marketing budgets while she audited our existing spend. That delayed our new purchase order to the marketing vendor, so potential leads sat on the wayside until we could resume our contract.

Chapter 14 Metrics: Putting it Together

Fix Facebook Ad Views

Facebook ad revenue went down 10% last week. What happened? And how would you fix it?

Things to Consider

- Start with brainstorming potential reasons, using either the AARM or E5 framework.
- Next, identify the root cause.
- Finally, make recommendations on how to address the issue.

Common Mistakes

- Not using a metric framework, which makes it harder to brainstorm a list of potential root causes.
- Not giving the interviewer a roadmap, making the answer hard to follow.

Answer

CANDIDATE: Give me a few seconds to collect my thoughts.

INTERVIEWER: Sure.

Candidate takes seven seconds.

CANDIDATE: Here is how I want to approach the question:

1. Brainstorm a list of potential reasons
2. Identify the root cause
3. Brainstorm ways to fix
4. Make a recommendation

INTERVIEWER: That's a sound plan. Go for it.

CANDIDATE: Give me a moment to brainstorm reasons why ad revenue might be down.

Candidates takes 30 seconds.

CANDIDATE: Okay, here's what I came up with:

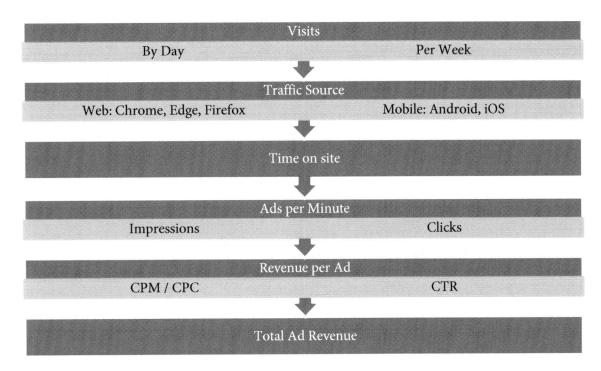

INTERVIEWER: Interesting. Walk me through it.

CANDIDATE: When it comes to total ad revenue, there are really two primary drivers: number of ads shown and the revenue per ad. If you don't have a preference, I'll start with the drivers that affect the number of ads shown.

INTERVIEWER: Okay.

CANDIDATE: The first thing I'd ask: have there any significant week over week changes in visits?

ITNERVIEWER. No.

CANDDIATE: How about any differences in traffic type? Mix shift from web to mobile? Or mix shift from iOS to Android?

INTERVIEWER: Why would that affect revenue?

CANDIDATE: Ad rates might differ based on platform. For example, advertisers prefer to pay more for web vs. mobile ads. Web have higher commercial value as most people do not complete ecommerce transactions on a mobile device: it's hard to type. Just imagine entering address and credit card details on a tiny smartphone.

INTERVIEWER: I see that you've written down traffic by browser type. Why would we care if someone were using Google Chrome vs. Microsoft Edge?

CANDIDATE: The behavior of a Google Chrome user is different from a Microsoft Edge user. Since Chrome is usually not pre-installed by default on Windows or Mac, Google Chrome users are more tech savvy; they have to go through extra effort to download and install the Chrome browser to their machine. More tech savvy users are more likely to avoid ads.

INTERVIEWER: Okay. Let's say there are no differences in traffic source.

CANDIDATE: How about time on site?

INTERVIEWER: Why would time on site go down?

CANDIDATE: Sometimes time on site can go down due to seasonality. Other times time on site can go down when there's a bug that prevents the user from using our products effectively.

INTERVIEWER: Let's say it's none of those.

CANDIDATE: How about revenue per ad?

INTERVIEWER: Revenue per ad is definitely down.

CANDIDATE: Is it because our CPMs or CPCs are down?

INTERVIEWER: No perceptible changes there.

CANDDIATE: So then a CTR impact?

INTERVIEWER: Yes, CTRs are down.

CANDIDATE: Is there a reason why CTRs are down?

INTERVIEWER: What are some potential explanations for a decreased CTR?

CANDIDATE: Give me a few seconds to brainstorm some ideas.

Candidate takes 20 seconds.

CANDIDATE: I came up with a couple of ideas on why CTR may be down:

1. Client-side suppression of ads, with the use of ad blockers, can lead to reduced CTRs.
2. Ad inventory may have changed. There's a higher percentage of less clicky ads than before.
3. User behavior may have changed. Users are getting smarter about not clicking ads.
4. Ad layout or placement may have changed, especially if the size of the ad changed or if the ad moved to the bottom.

INTERVIEWER: You got it. The ad inventory changed. We banned an advertiser that was promoting weight loss supplements. The ad claims were grossly inflated, and consumers complained about the advertiser's landing page experience.

CANDIDATE: Good to know.

INTERVIEWER: So how would you address the issue? Let's say the executives aren't happy with the revenue drop

CANDIDDATE: Here are some ideas I have from the top of my head on how to increase ad revenue:

1. **Get more advertisers**. This increases supply and competition, pushing up bid prices.
2. **Get existing advertisers to advertise more**. We can ask existing advertisers to increase budgets or expand targeting parameters.
3. **Increase ad quality**. We can ask advertisers to make their ads more compelling, increasing the likelihood that users will click on their ads and / or convert.
4. **Improve landing page experience**. We can ask advertisers to improve their landing page experience. If the landing page experience improves, those advertisers will more likely get more conversions. If the conversion results improve, then advertisers will more likely pay more for advertising.

INTERVIEWER: Well done.

Photo Filter Signups

You are the marketing analytics manager for a small startup that allows users to apply a filter to user-recorded videos.

Signups went up 4,000% vs. the 30-day average. What happened? And how would you maintain that momentum?

Things to Consider

- Big spikes are more common for a newer product with a small customer base.

Common Mistakes

- Forgetting that signups can be affected by download to signup conversion rate.
- Not knowing what factors affect downloads from an app store like iTunes.

Answer

CANDIDATE: Four thousand percent?

INTERVIEWER: Yep.

CANDIDATE: Okay, here's how I would approach the situation:

1. Brainstorm a list of potential reasons
2. Identify the root cause
3. Brainstorm ways to fix
4. Make a recommendation

INTERVIEWER: Okay.

CANDIDATE: Give me a moment to brainstorm a couple of reasons.

Candidates takes 30 seconds.

CANDIDATE: Okay, here's what I came up with:

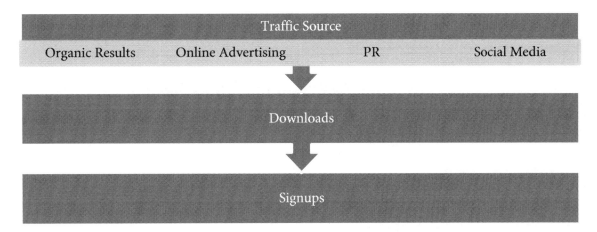

Let's start with the bottom and work backwards. First, were there any conversion rate changes from downloads to signups?

INTERVIEWER: Nope, conversion rates held steady and doesn't explain the increase in traffic.

CANDDIATE: Okay, if the conversion rate held steady, then I'll have to assume that signups increased because downloads increased.

INTERVIEWER: Yes.

CANDIDATE: Four levers come to mind that affect downloads:

1. Organic results in the iTunes or Google Play store
2. Online advertising
3. Social media
4. PR

Did I miss any?

INTERVIEWER: What affects iTunes store downloads?

CANDIDATE: Here are a few things to come to mind:

1. Keyword relevancy
2. Reviews
3. App description
4. App screenshots
5. App icon

INTERVIEWER: Good list. Let's say you haven't missed any levers. What next?

CANDIDATE: Speaking of iTunes store downloads, did the number of referrals from the iTunes or Google Play store change?

INTERVIEWER: No.

CANDIDATE: How about social media?

INTERVIEWER: There was a change there. We got a substantial increase in referrals from a French website.

CANDIDATE: What kind of website was it?

INTERVIEWER: It's a large community of hip-hop dancers.

CANDIDATE: So a community member mentioned the app in the forums?

INTERVIEWER: Yes. They love how the app could record their dance videos and make them look like they were professionally edited.

CANDIDATE: Great. My next mission is to figure out how we can replicate this elsewhere. I have two main ideas:

1. Identify other hip-hop communities around the world and promote our app with those communities.
2. Find other performance communities, such as skateboarders and ballet dancers, which would be interested in using our app to capture, modify and share their experiences.

INTERVIEWER: So you would just spam the community boards and beg them to use the app?

CANDIDATE: No, we'd have to be more thoughtful than that. They are likely to be skeptical of commercial messages, especially from someone who just appeared in the community overnight. We'd have to:

- Identify the key influencers
- Develop a relationship with those influencers
- Demonstrate our app
- Help them use the app and offer incredible customer service

After we've helped influencers through those stages, then we'll increase our chances of getting an authentic endorsement in their communities.

INTERVIEWER: How about if the influencers try our software and hate it? Wouldn't we have wasted our time?

CANDDIATE: Actually, I don't see it that way. Even if we don't get an endorsement, it'll be a chance to get feedback on our app, which we can use to inform our product roadmap. Improving the product is just as important as getting the word out. Better yet, if we later tell the influencer, "Hey, we heard your feedback and improved the product," they might be flattered that we respected their opinion and took action on their feedback.

INTERVIEWER: Good point.

Chapter 15 Hypothetical: Opinion

House Pricing

Zillow's price estimation tool depends on the following pieces of data: property tax history, comparable houses and finalized sales details from counties. How does this dependency impact price estimation?

Things to Consider

- Historical data lags the current reality.
- Reported information may be incorrect.
- Comparisons with neighborhood houses may be flawed, especially if those houses have interior upgrades or downgrades that aren't reflected in the price.
- Not all counties report finalized sales details.

Common Mistakes

- Being hasty.
- Feeling unnecessarily anxious because of unfamiliarity with real estate valuation.

Answer

CANDIDATE: Let's walk through all three.

- **Property Tax History.** There might be a lot of things that would cause you extra taxes if you own this house. Some examples may include solar panels and things like how likely is the house going to be flooded or is it likely to be damaged during an earthquake. This probably factors into your insurance too.
- **Comparable Houses.** People who buy houses typically take a couple of months, and definitely look at a lot of houses. They tend to know what they want, and will compare your house with similar houses. By that logic, you can't price it too high or too low compared to another house.
- **Finalized Sales Details.** Just because your house is priced this way doesn't mean it'll actually sell this much, especially in places like California where the housing prices are crazy. It's not uncommon to attach an extra 10-15% on the price as the final sale.

Basically, these all affect price estimation. As Zillow, our job is to provide an accurate data to the user. By including these we do a better job at presenting the real possibility to a user, saving them time and providing a better user experience.

INTERVIEWER: Could you think of examples where these data could skew the actual price?

CANDIDATE: Hmm, that could definitely happen. For example, you might see a house that sells for quite a bit during the summer, but a lot less on a comparable house in the same neighborhood during winter. This is because more people tend to want to buy houses during summer. Also, these data need to be updated annually, because house prices change a lot in places like California. It may not matter in places like Georgia where the price is less fluid.

INTERVIEWER: Is there any way you can prevent skewing?

CANDIDATE: We could, for example, weed out the top 1% and the bottom 1%. These might be outliers.

Competitive Move

Tell me about a competitor's move in the past six months. What do you think about it?

Things to Consider

- The interviewer is gauging your industry knowledge.
- They also want you to demonstrate that your passion for the industry.

Common Mistakes

- Failing to do your homework on key industry trends in the last few months.
- Bringing up a dated, commonplace competitive trend.

Answer

CANDIDATE: Nintendo recently announced that they would launch games on non-Nintendo mobile devices such as the iPhone and Android. This move cannibalizes Nintendo's pre-existing revenue stream selling their own handheld devices like the DS and games.

This is even more shocking considered the strategic advantage of owning the platform: the gaming platform owner receives royalties not only on games that they publish but also royalties that third-parties publish as well. With this new arrangement, Nintendo would now have to pay a $0.30 royalty to Apple and Google for every $1 they make.

Despite the cannibalization and the now departed strategic advantage, I believe there is some upside for Nintendo including:

- **New Market.** They are going to tap on a lot of new people who don't own or plan to own a Nintendo handheld device. This increases their potential customer audience. Last time I checked, Nintendo has sold 154 million DS units, of which 20 million are of the latest generation. There are 2 billion smartphone users worldwide. This is a significantly larger market.
- **New customers are incremental**. Mobile phone gamers and DS gamers do not overlap. DS gamers that pay $200 for a handheld gaming device is not a casual gamer. Most mobile phone gamers, however, are casual gamers. And to make it even better, a Nintendo game loyalist will likely play games on both mobile phone and DS platforms, especially if some Nintendo games are not available on both platforms.

Favorite Excel Function

What's your favorite Excel function?

Things to Consider

- Using a casual question, the interviewer is testing your Excel proficiency.
- The interviewer wants to feel smarter, so it's best to share an Excel function that he or she is not familiar with.
- If that's not possible, choose an Excel function that most people would consider is an advanced function. Some potential ideas: VLOOKUP, Autofill and Transpose.

Common Mistakes

- Choosing Pivot Tables, a popular feature that's selected by most candidates.
- Having difficulty explaining a complicated feature in an easy-to-understand way such as regression analysis.

Answer

CANDIDATE: I love Excel's data table feature.

INTERVIEWER: Tables?

CANDIDATE: Yes, data tables. Unlike tables in Microsoft Word, Excel's data tables feature allows a user to calculate multiple results.

INTERVIEWER: I'm not sure if I follow.

CANDIDATE: Let's say I'm the product manager for Tesla's soon-to-be released electric SUV. When putting together my revenue projection, I want to develop a best, average and worst case scenario by varying adoption rates. I also want to vary the list price. If I had 5 different list prices and 5 different adoption rates, that's 25 models I'd have to create. That's a lot of work.

INTERVIEWER: Not to mention potential for manual errors.

CANDIDATE: Exactly. So with data tables, I can input a range of adoption rates as well as list prices. And Excel would spit out 25 revenue estimates in one-step.

INTERVIEWER. Save time and minimize errors.

CANDIDATE: Bingo.

Startup Dictator

If you were appointed as dictator of your previous startup, what would you change?

Things to Consider

- Use the McKinsey situation, complication and resolution framework.

Common Mistakes

- Use this question as an opportunity to vent, blame and/or point fingers. As a result, the negative tone makes the candidate sound bitter.
- Getting caught up with complaining that the candidate forgets to answer the question "what would you change?"

Answer

Situation

I'm not proud of the situation, but our startup had to shut down three months ago. It stings a lot given how much I cared for the company and how much time I put into it. Even worse, one of our top competitors was ultimately acquired for $250 million. That makes it hurt so much more.

Complications

There are three reasons why our startup failed.

1. **Terrible product with a long setup time**. On the one hand, our solution required 15 to 20 minutes of setup time. On the other hand, our competitor's setup required just two minutes. Our competitor had a whopping 30 million customers whereas we had just 2 million. And to make matters worse, their product was free.
2. **Poor branding**. The name of our website was called SalesTreats.com. I didn't like the name, but we told ourselves that the name didn't matter as long as we had a great product. Well, our company's name sounded ridiculous, and it was hard for anyone to take us seriously.
3. **Didn't know how to filter the noise**. We started to do things because our investors wanted us to. As a result, we strayed from our original vision, which customers loved. I wish we were more willing to say no to our investors.

Resolution

In retrospect, there are three things I wish we had done:

1. **Make a bigger push to acquire the domain Sales.com**. We explored it initially, but we were scared away by the $3 million offer price. We preempted our search by saying it was more important to focus and prioritize product over a memorable name.

2. **Focus on customers**. I would spend more time researching customer needs and prototyping. I felt our startup was solving a big problem, but we were too busy building to truly understand what our customers wanted.

3. **Reduce reliance on investors**. We spent a lot of money just so we could keep up with other Bay Area startups. We splurged on an expensive SF office location, employee perks and high salaries. I wish we would have forgone some of those choices to keep our burn rate down, reducing our dependence on investors so that we could maintain stronger customer focus.

4. **Improve product onboarding**. Our product was too onerous. In retrospect, I would have gladly paid the $500k per year to have a third-party vendor integrate with our customer's sales systems. It would have provided a much better onboarding system that would have minimized the amount of typing our users had to do.

Superpower

What is your superpower?

Things to Consider

- This is a more casual way of asking, "Why makes you stand out from other candidates?"
- Think about your personal brand. That is, after the interview is over, how do you want to be remembered by the interviewers?
- Based on that decision, choose a superpower that's related and reinforces your personal brand.
- Creativity counts. Clever and witty responses will be particularly noteworthy.

Common Mistakes

- Choosing a superpower that's bland and boring.

Answer

CANDIDATE: My superpower is able to multi-task really well. This is true both in my professional and personal life. I am always juggling multiple things at once.

For my work, since I am in a startup, I am juggling multiple roles at once, and handling a lot of different tasks every day. For example, on a daily basis, I have to get in a strategy meeting with other co-founders, I have to work with marketing on our next CPI campaigns, I have to look at data for the ongoing projects (and I am handling 3 right now). I have to work with the development team on the next update. I then still have to talk with the customer service team, art team, other product managers, and business development. Realistically, I'd like to section my day off for each task, but that never happens as something demands my immediately attention so I end up juggling multiple tasks at once.

For my personal life, I do this quite a bit too. I guess it got carried over from my work and I live my life like a PM. I end up doing a lot of things at once, like talking to my parents while driving to get groceries or making plans with my friends while grocery shopping. Even when I am relaxing, I am playing games with Netflix playing on my right monitor and my chat going on my left monitor while being on TeamSpeak. This also ends up quite helping me while playing games too, since I can manage multiple things at once.

Starting a Company

If you could start a company with $1,000,000 right now what would it be? Why?

Things to Consider

The interviewer is testing your business judgment and your ability to articulate a business case.

Common Mistakes

Giving a personal entrepreneurial goal such as opening a restaurant or starting a band.

Answer

CANDIDATE: If I started a company today, I'd start Uber for trucking. That is, transport heavy materials for businesses where drivers would be available on-demand. There's a couple reasons why this is a compelling market:

- **Big market**. In 2014, the trucking industry netted over $700 billion.
- **Fragmented**. There are 1.2 million trucking companies in the US, and most of them have fewer than six trucks.
- **Well-suited for on-demand coordination**. A fair amount of trucking comes from short-notice shipments.

It's also attractive to me personally. First, I spent my summers in Evansville, Indiana working at my father and uncle's moving company. Naturally, creating a business that reminds me of my childhood brings back fond memories. Second, my father and uncle have mentioned their interest in having me take over the family business. I'm excited about the opportunity because it merges my passion for technology and a family business that I know well.

Dealing with Defeat

How do you deal with defeat?

Things to Consider

- Use the Rule of Three.
- Offer an example to demonstrate that you behave in accordance with what you normally do.
- Include emotions to make the story more humanistic, increasing your chances of connecting and establishing rapport.

Common Mistakes

- Not offering an example, which makes the answer sound textbook and conventional.
- Giving an answer that's too short, leaving the interviewer wanting more.

Answer

CANDIDATE: When dealing with defeat, I usually go through three phases:

- **Accept failure**. I could let it impact me for days, or I can resume my life. It's not easy to be positive, but I try to be resilient and bounce back quickly.
- **Learn**. Failure is an opportunity to learn. Did I make a careless mistake? Could I have avoided it? What could I have done differently? There's nothing worse than repeating the same mistake, so I log all the insights and takeaways that I can.
- **Move forward**. I think about what my next goal should be and create a new challenge for myself.

Would it help if I shared a story about a time when I dealt with defeat?

INTERVIEWER: Sure, go for it.

CANDIDATE: This past July, I joined Google's cloud team as technical program manager. Two weeks into the job, I got a call from Ileana; she said, "Amber, there's a production workload that you created with no billing ID. Do you know what's going on?"

I immediately felt a little flush and embarrassed. I stammered, "Uh, I'll look into it." After investigation, I realized that I didn't attach a billing ID to a customer workload that I created. I did the quick math; that's $30,000 revenue that Google missed out on.

At that point, I had three options:

1. Deny that the mistake happened and blame it on the poorly designed software. Or perhaps even accuse Ileana.
2. Complain to my boss that they should not have a new person take a critical task.
3. Accept the mistake and learn from it.

In the heat of the moment, options 1 and 2 were not as unreasonable as they sound. I've seen my co-workers deny or complain often. And quite frankly, I was tired of being the "good one."

But I decided to accept my mistake and learn from it. Within the next couple of days, I created a new UI wireframe that would prevent me and others from forgetting the billing ID again. I also made a suggestion on how to streamline the process so that new workloads could be created in 40% less time.

One year later, during my one-year anniversary, I received a promotion. My boss teased me about my $30,000 mistake from a year ago. But he remarked that's part of the reason why I got the promotion: I was a role model for others on the team on how to recover from a mistake AND improve the company for the better.

Dealing with Complex Problems

Could you deal with complex problems?

Things to Consider

- Don't let the awkward phrasing unnerve you.
- Don't take advantage of the poorly phrased question with a curt "yes." Performing well at the interview is your responsibility. Good candidates know that curt responses are unsatisfactory and damage their chances of getting an offer.

Common Mistakes

- Responding to the odd phrasing with an inelegant response like, "That doesn't make any sense. Of course I can deal with complex problems."

Answer

CANDIDATE: That's a really open-ended question. Do you have any specifics?

INTERVIEWER: It's open-ended on purpose.

CANDIDATE: When I deal with a complex problem, I take a divide and conquer approach. That is, I would break down a complex problem into base components. Then, I analyze each component individually. Lastly, I check each component to arrive at the issue's root cause.

INTERVIEWER: Can you give me a personal example of a time when you used this approach?

CANDIDATE: Yes, this happened last week. Our users complained that our game caused them to lose too many chips. That's an open-ended complaint. While it doesn't sound complex, the complaint forced me to think about the internal mechanics of the game to determine what went wrong. So I decided to divide and conquer the problem.

First, I isolated the problem to a specific game mode since we have five different game modes. After pinpointing the correct game mode, I wanted to isolate which part would cause a loss of chips. I sifted through multiple issues including UX structure, input, labels and actions.

Eventually I pinpointed the problem. I asked the engineers to pull log data, which confirmed a minor bug in our game. We fixed the bug and released a patch the following week.

Getting up in the Morning

If you get up in the morning and you feel really bad, what motivates you to start the day?

Things to Consider

- Use the Rule of Three.
- Interviewers are looking for whether you tried to understand why you feel bad, how you addressed it, and did you have the resiliency to push through it.

Common Mistakes

- Not coming up with creative ways to get motivated.
- Suffering through the pain alone and not getting others to help.

Answer

CANDIDATE: I can think of three things:

- **Customers.** Our product services many customers, and if I don't get up and fix our problems for the day, they will be disappointed. As a PM, customers represent our true north. They are the lifeblood of the company. Without them, we have nothing.
- **Team.** As a PM, I feel responsible for my team. They expect me to do my job right everyday as much as I expect them to do the same. They have my back and I have theirs. If I don't get up and do my share, I am betraying that camaraderie.
- **Goal.** I keep our goal in mind whenever I feel bad. As a PM, it's my job to point to the true north. I must keep our goal in mind. If I don't get up, we will not progress toward that goal today.

To conclude, if I feel really bad, I think about our customers, my team, and our goal.

Chapter 16 Hypothetical: Problem Solving

CEO of Showrooms and Physical Distributors

A lighting company CEO has a long tradition of working with showrooms and physical distributors, what do we say about their perception that Amazon poses a threat to their business?

Things to Consider

- Why do you think the lighting company CEO would be threatened?
- What can Amazon do that can be beneficial for the CEO? Think win-win.

Common Mistakes

- Automatically assume that the issue is about money and unilaterally offering discounts when the problem could have been solved differently.

Answer

CANDIDATE: I would first say that Amazon naturally has a disadvantage when it comes to products that do better in showrooms. Take things like selling a kitchen counter, for example. People like to match big pieces like this with the rest of their house, and a lot of it also depends on how it would look like once it's in place. Amazon can't really showcase it that well on the Internet.

I would then talk about how Amazon probably won't even sell bigger pieces like this, because typically these things are purchased from brick-and-mortar stores. They would require installations, which Amazon doesn't usually do. Another thing is that Amazon usually only ship small to medium size packages. These would be huge.

Finally, I would talk about how online buyers and people who purchase in brick-and-mortar stores are really two separate groups. Most people that shop online don't want to go out to a brick-and-mortar store in the first place, that's why they are buying stuff online. So really, his business and Amazon aren't even competing..

Chapter 17 Strategy: New Market Entry

Google Store

If you could open a Google store anywhere, where would it be and why?

Things to Consider

- "Google store" is an ambiguous term. What does it mean? Something equivalent to Microsoft or Apple stores? Or is it just a merchandising store?
- What's the goal of a Google store? Brand awareness? Sales? Support? All of the above?
- How does your proposed location maximize the target objectives?

Common Mistakes

- Not clarifying Google store.
- Suggesting a fancy location such as New York City's Times Square or London's Piccadilly Circus without understanding or explaining the reasoning behind it.

Answer

CANDIDATE: Are we talking about a physical store? Like Microsoft or Apple stores?

INTERVIEWER: Yes.

CANDIDATE: Am I safe to assume it would showcase things like the latest Nexus, Chromebooks, and Google subsidiary products like Nest.

INTERVIEWER: Yep, that sounds about right.

CANDIDATE: I would open Google stores in China. There are three reasons:

- **New Market:** China is a new market for Google. Its market is filled with a lot of different Android products. Google Nexus is not one of them. Also, Chromebooks and such are not available in China.
- **Showrooming:** China has a lot of people, and even though e-commerce is a huge thing (one would argue it's more popular there than here), it's also a country with a huge population. Having stores there would certainly attract crowds, and devices tend to sell better when people can play with them anyway.
- **Getting around the Ban:** Google Search and Google Play are banned in China. There could be potential getting around that. At the very least we can increase Google's branding in China.

INTERVIEWER: If you have to pick one, what is the most important reason?

CANDIDATE: I would say new market. China has one of the world's largest markets, and Google really needs to get in on that. There are going to be a lot of difficulties, but I think it'll be well worth it.

Expanding UberPool

We're about to expand UberPool. What cities should we expand to?

Things to Consider

- Which cities have had the most success with UberPool? And what explains the success?
- What best practices and pitfalls have been gleaned so far?
- Which cities are most likely to duplicate the success of accomplished UberPool cities?

Common Mistakes

- Failed to think through what conditions contribute to UberPool's success.

Answer

CANDIDATE: I would say any cities that are crowded. Of the top of my head, cities like Beijing, Shanghai, Guangzhou, Mumbai, New Delhi, Tokyo, etc. I am not sure if any of these already have UberPool. The reasons why I picked them is because:

- **Less Waiting.** We will have a problem picking up people, since you have to wade through traffic, but since you generally pick up people close to each other, it won't be as bad. You also tend to carry people who are going to destinations that are close to each other. This way there will be less cars picking up people and dropping people off, meaning that it will be faster.
- **Less Traffic.** Since fewer cars will go from point A to point B (points being big zones), there are bound to be fewer cars on important highways and freeways. This means less traffic.
- **Lower Cost.** In a city with a lot of traffic, there are bound to be a lot of alternatives that are cheaper and faster, like subways or buses. UberPool and its lower price can compete with these alternatives.

INTERVIEWER: Wouldn't UberPool being stuck in traffic contribute to a bad user experience?

CANDIDATE: This is a two-part question. On one hand, we have people who have to wait longer to get picked up and dropped off because of carpooling. On the other, we have people who have to wade through heavy traffic to get somewhere. Both of these situations are going to happen regardless of whether or not they are using UberPool instead of regular Uber, so it's unavoidable unless we come up with UberBus or something similar, so it's not really a factor we need to consider.

And if you think about it, UberPool will actually make pickup and drop-off faster. When people asked to get picked up or dropped off, there are generally certain locations that are really popular. Typically, there aren't going to be enough cars in those spots (although a lot of drivers will wait around there because they know these are popular spots). By carpooling, cars can pick up a lot of people easily because you are realistically all waiting for one car instead of everyone waiting for multiple cars. This speeds up the process because having one car wade through traffic is better than, say, 3 or 4 cars because then you are contributing to the traffic problem.

Google Maps in Mongolia

How would you release Google Maps in Mongolia?

Things to Consider

- Do you have PR and regulatory staff to deal with issues?
- Do you have operations and customer support staff to handle in coming additions, editions and deletions to map information?
- Would Google Maps have to be adapted to Mongolian customs or unique Mongolian technology infrastructure?

Common Mistakes

- Assuming Mongolia is identical to the country that the candidate is most familiar with.

Answer

CANDIDATE: I would first wonder if it is worthwhile to set up Google Maps there. I would imagine it is not exactly a hot tourist attraction and not a lot of people live there either. I believe there are a lot of underdeveloped areas in Mongolia; most of the people live around Ulan Bator, the capital city.

I would first consider if we have good enough Internet access there. Is there high smartphone and computer penetration? While a lot of underdeveloped areas means it's easy to get lost and Google Maps would be handy, it also might mean a lot of bad signals. I also don't find it appealing to "street view" the plains of Mongolia.

It is unlikely there is a local company we can partner with, but it cannot hurt to check. Mongolia is an untapped market I, but I am not sure its potential is that great. Given the uncertain potential, perhaps we can assign this project to Google's Chinese or Russian offices to minimize additional investment.

Both offices have advantages. Google Russia is fluent in Russian, a language many Mongolians speak. However, Google China is geographically closer to China.

Chapter 18 Strategy: Other

Cutting a Google Product

Which Google product would you cut and why?

Things to Consider

- Create criteria on what makes a product worth cutting vs. one that is not.
- Do a discernably comprehensive analysis on why your cut proposal makes sense.
- Make sure your analysis is balanced to make it feel both comprehensive and believable.

Common Mistakes

- Missing a critical factor such as revenue, cost, customer, competitor or employee impact.
- Being fearful that the interviewer would disagree with a strong recommendation, so avoid making a recommendation or make a safe recommendation

Answer

CANDIDATE: I would cut out Google+ because of three reasons:

- **Nothing happens.** Nothing ever happens on Google+. Why? Two reasons:
  - Facebook is good enough, and Google+ isn't perceived to be better.
  - Users didn't actively signup for Google+. Instead, Google automatically created Google+ accounts for its Gmail users.
- **Inhibits other Google products.** By requiring all Google products to integrate with Google+, products have gotten worse. For example, YouTube user access and permission levels are awkward to use, in large part due to a forced Google+ integration. Instead, YouTube should have adopted industry standard sign-in systems like Facebook and Twitter login.
- **Hurts Google's reputation.** Because of the Google+ fiasco, Google is now perceived as:
  - Trying too hard to win.
  - Not caring about the user's experience.
  - Failing to innovate, primarily because Google's interface looks similar to Facebook's.

INTERVIEWER: So what's your solution to Google's desire to win in social networking?

CANDIDATE: I don't have the silver bullet solution. If it was that easy, Google would have done it already. But here are some things I'd explore:

- **Focus on areas of strength**. Google Hangouts is a very popular byproduct of the Google+ effort. It brought group video conferencing to the web. Can they do it for mobile too?
- **Consider new segments**. How about social networking apps for specific personas? For example:
  - Professionals scenarios
    - Social networking for dentists: share photos of symptoms that the dentist can't diagnose
    - Social networking for lawyers: a question and answer site for uncommon legal questions

- o Non-professional scenarios
  - Social networking for moms: share recommendations for child care, summer camps, dentists
  - Social network for recreational sports enthusiasts: help players of team sports find users for a local basketball, football, softball or tennis game
- **Focus on new mediums**. There are lots of new computing platforms beyond mobile including virtual reality (Oculus and Google Glass), Internet of Things (e.g. thermostats, security cameras, and garage door openers), and drones. There's a need for social networking here, and Google could establish a first mover advantage here.

Multiple Starbucks

Why does Starbucks expand the way they do having multiple stores next to each other?

Things to Consider

- Ask for time to pause and think. It's likely that the interviewer has reason(s) in mind. You will get dinged if you do not guess his or her specific reasons. Even if you happen to not guess his or her reasons, the interviewer is more likely to forgive you if you've got a long list of five to ten reasons.
- To spur brainstorming, use a strategy checklist like Porter's Five Forces.

Common Mistakes

- Getting flustered.
- Brainstorming a short list.
- Missing important reasons.

Answer

CANDIDATE: Can I brainstorm a bit?

Candidate takes one minute.

CANDIDATE: I can think of a few reasons:

- **No room for expansion.** Maybe the Starbucks is located at a busy and desirable location, like downtown SF. It may not feasible to knock down a wall and expand into a nearby room.
- **Branding.** If you walk into a busy part of town and you see multiple Starbucks all on the same street, there's a huge branding effect. It more strongly reinforces the perception that coffee = Starbucks, just like online search = Google.
- **Defensive Play.** If it's a good section of town, other coffee shops might move in. If Starbucks gobbles up good real estate, their competitors will have a harder time moving in.
- **Lower Buyer Power.** If Starbucks is the only coffee supplier in single vicinity, that means customers have fewer choices. If customers have fewer choices, then Starbucks can more easily get customers to accept price increases.
- **Lower Supplier Power.** By the same reasoning, if local suppliers only have the option of selling to Starbucks, Starbucks can negotiate better prices with their local suppliers, since those suppliers are dependent on Starbucks for a majority of their revenue.

Strategic Analysis of Microsoft

Do a strategic analysis of a Microsoft business.

Things to Consider

- Did you use a strategy framework such as SWOT analysis or Porter's Five Forces as a checklist to organize your thoughts?

Common Mistakes

- Limited insight and analysis depth because the candidate chose to analyze several businesses vs. a single business.
- Didn't use a strategy framework to organize thoughts, which led to the analysis feeling incomplete and unsatisfying

Answer

CANDIDATE: Microsoft is split down to two parts, basically, one customer facing and one enterprise facing. This is prevalent in pretty much all of its services:

- **Windows.** Microsoft's operating system. It's the core of Microsoft. It has over 90% market domination and a stream of unending users. Consumers and enterprises play a huge part. Consumers get home solutions and enterprises can get professional and server solutions.
- **Office.** Big part of Microsoft is the Office Suite. It's pretty much required for both consumer and professional settings.
- **Azure & Visual Studio.** These two are pretty closely knitted, and offer enterprise solutions.
- **Microsoft Edge.** Microsoft's own web browser.
- **Bing & MSN.** Microsoft's web services, which is promoted heavily by Windows through Microsoft Edge. Mostly consumer based, but Bing has its own ads which is enterprise facing, and translation services which can be enterprise facing.
- **Skype.** Consumer and enterprise facing communications software.
- **Outlook / Hotmail.** Email client, consumer and enterprise facing.
- **Windows Phone.** Mostly for consumers. This also includes the Windows Store, which is available on both the phone and Windows. This also includes Surface and other tablets.
- **Xbox.** Consumers. Platform for games. A lot of developer support and first party developers too.
- **Innovation.** Microsoft has a lot of innovative teams, such as HoloLens.

The gist of it is that Microsoft has a strong business team that has connections with pretty much most of the enterprise world. Windows is powering a lot of services in both consumer and enterprise. This allows the core audience to experience other products as Microsoft promotes them through Windows.

Microsoft also supports providing a lot of its tools to students for free through Spark, which means they are more likely to choose companies that work with Microsoft services which keeps the enterprise cycle going strong.

Games are also huge for Windows, and Microsoft has a strong relationship with developers to make sure they keep dominating the PC gaming market.

Microsoft also works with a lot of hardware and software companies to keep Windows' market share strong.

Improving the Company

If you were the CEO of Microsoft, what would you change to improve the company?

Things to Consider

- What are the biggest threats to the company?
- What are the biggest opportunities?
- What are the core competencies that the company should leverage?
- What are ingrained consumer perceptions that the company should avoid?

Common Mistakes

- Taking a single product view vs. a company view.

Answer

CANDIDATE: Are you talking about the company culture or product?

INTERVIEWER: Anything related to the company, like culture, direction, etc.

CANDIDATE: Hmm, give me some time to brainstorm please.

Candidate takes one minute.

CANDIDATE: I think there are several things I would change about Microsoft.

- **Cool, Young Culture:** Microsoft currently has a bit of a traditional culture. Microsoft is an old company (in the tech space) and gives off the vibe that it's not really up with the times. Young people are a driving force behind innovation, and I think by adapting a younger and contemporary tech culture (like Google and Facebook) it would attract more talent.
- **Innovation:** Microsoft has its innovations, don't get me wrong, but it's not really well known for it, and definitely not in the league of Apple, Google or Facebook. Innovation is really the driving force behind revenue. I know most of Microsoft's revenue comes from the enterprise sector and innovation doesn't always make the biggest bucks, but Microsoft is losing out in a lot of emerging markets, and this is why. I mean, Google has driverless cars, Uber is tapping into a new market, and Airbnb is using a whole new model. Microsoft doesn't have anything equivalent.
- **Consumer Focused:** Like I said before, Microsoft is really focused on the enterprise sector. I think we are losing out in a lot of markets precisely because they are consumer-oriented. I am talking about mobile, browser, and gaming consoles. These are also new markets, and they tend to attract younger crowds. By shifting Microsoft into a more consumer-focused approach it would benefit us in the long run.

INTERVIEWER: To be consumer focused, you are saying Microsoft should move away from enterprise, where we make most of our revenue, and go for the consumer space? What if this change failed?

CANDIDATE: I am not saying we should move away from enterprise. Think of enterprise as a stable base. We are trying to expand and get another base. The world of tech constantly changes and new trends and markets

148

emerge. These are up for grabs, but only for the quickest and most innovative. A lot of the newer ones are consumer-based. By looking at the ones Microsoft isn't doing well in, we are seeing that they are mostly consumer based. So we should work on this.

Google vs. Microsoft

How would you re-position Google's offerings to counteract competitive threats from Microsoft?

Things to Consider

- Where do Microsoft and Google compete?
- Which Microsoft products represent the biggest threats to Google?
- Which perceptions are the most difficult for Google to change (e.g. privacy)?

Common Mistakes

- Suggesting boring ideas with limited effectiveness such as changing price or doing more marketing promotion

Answer

CANDIDATE: By offering, do you mean launching new products or are you talking more about directions?

INTERVIEWER: What new directions would you say Google should approach?

CANDIDATE: Hmm, I need to first think about Microsoft's competitive threats in order to consider those. Let me have some time to brainstorm.

Candidate takes one minute.

CANDIDATE: I can think of three threats Microsoft has competitively over Google:

- **Browser.** Microsoft is able to promote Microsoft Edge because it comes bundled with Windows. Chrome is winning now, mostly because of Android, but Microsoft will always have this threat looming over our head.
- **Enterprise Solutions.** I am talking about things like emails and servers. Microsoft has a lot of products devoted to them, and decades of enterprise relations.
- **Developer Tools.** Microsoft has a lot of developer tools, and they offer them free for students (Microsoft Spark). Visual Studio has become the de facto IDE for a lot of people.

Now with these in mind, I can think of directions we should head as Google:

- **OS.** Google is already doing this to some degree with Chromebooks, but it's not enough. One of the greatest strengths of Windows is its user base, which causes developers to develop for it which in turns drives more users. Google needs to focus on this.
- **Enterprise Solutions.** Google offers a lot of similar services (e.g. Gmail, Google Drive, Google Cloud), but it's the sales and business aspect that's letting Microsoft win. We need stronger business teams that work with enterprises.

- **Developer Tools.** Google is sort of doing this now, but it's not enough. Microsoft has been on the horizon for so many years and Microsoft Spark is so good at converting students into permanent Microsoft users. Google needs to focus more on schools.

So by examining all three potential threats, we see that Google should really focus more on relations. Google has all the necessary tools and products, but because Microsoft has either already taken the market share or has an excellent business relations team, Microsoft is winning out in these areas.

Google's Strategy

What is Google's strategy?

Things to Consider

- How does Google make money?
- What are the key assets that Google has invented to feed its business model?
- How does Google prevent its business model from getting obsolete?

Common Mistakes

- Not following the revenue model to discover the company's strategy

Answer

CANDIDATE: Google's strategy really focuses on getting lots and lots of users. Google makes products that are innovative and convenient which tends to attract a lot of early adopters and ends up snowballing to become a huge business on its own. We see this with Gmail, Google Maps, and Google Drive.

Google Search remains its core component, of course, and was what started it all. By making a lot of products like this, it allows Google to build based on its strengths. For example, think of Gmail. It was first built because Google Search was already popular. A cross promotion then happened and a lot of users were introduced to Gmail. Gmail then made a lot of people own an account, which fed back into Search because now data can be tracked to users. Both of these worked together to make advertisement better.

This is the reason why Google seems unstoppable in making new products, because everything is building on its strengths, and then goes back and enhances existing products.

In the beginning, most of Google's revenue comes from advertisement, with Search, Gmail, and YouTube leading the way. Google then begins to diversify its business, venturing into other things like Nest, Fiber, and selfless driving cars. This goes back to the building upon its strength and huge user base I talked about earlier. Because Google has the financial backing, brand recognition, and huge user base, it's able to expand into new businesses that tie in to previous businesses and grow the company.

Analysis of Google Acquisitions

Give your analysis of several recent acquisitions that Google has made.

Things to Consider

- List at least three acquisitions to indicate your passion for the company through your knowledge of company-related current events.
- A simple pro and con analysis could suffice.

Common Mistakes

- Mentioning only common reasons for acquisitions including revenue, patents or talent acquisition; ignoring other reasons including competitive defense, strategic learning or simply irrational behavior.

Answer

CANDIDATE: I can think of three recent acquisitions: Fly Labs for Google Photos, Tilt Brush and Thrive Audio.

Fly Labs has synergies with Google Photos. Fly Labs has over 3 million downloads globally. This is a smart move because Flickr is slowly dying, and with the rise of Imgur, it appears that photos are the next big social thing. Google+ is not working out well. By slowly improving and expanding Google Photos, it could become the next social powerhouse, especially with the number of users Google already has.

Tilt Brush is a 3-D painting application; it allows you to essentially paint a room like it's your canvas. This is a cool idea, but also the future. Google has been trying hard to introduce VR to the world. This makes it a natural expansion for Google. One of the early criticisms of VR is applications are limited. 3-D painting can be an killer application for early adopters.

Thrive Audio is like the Tilt Brush acquisition in many ways. It is positional audio designed with VR in mind. With this we are also seeing Google taking the lead in preparing for VR being the next big platform.

With these recent acquisitions, Google appears to be proving two points:

- Google is aware of its own shortcomings (e.g. social) and is seeking new ways to strengthen them.
- Google is preparing for a world where VR is the next big computing platform by keeping up with the VR moves of its two major competitors: Facebook and Microsoft.

Google Moonshot Projects

Why do you think Google is investing so much in its moonshot projects?

Things to Consider

- What is the impact of moonshot projects on the company?
- What is the impact on employees?
- What is the impact on competition?

Common Mistakes

- Not mentioning the need to attract and engage employees who desire challenging projects.
- Not stating the need to empower employees with a greater sense of freedom.

Answer

CANDIDATE: I think there are several reasons for this.

One, moonshots drive innovation. Remember 20% time? That was something most companies wouldn't have done, but Google did it. Amazing projects came out of 20% time including Gmail and Google News. Look at Gmail, for example. It is the most used email client in the world right now. Gmail alone probably made enough revenue to cover every 20% time ever spent. We can see why Google would encourage 20% time.

Two, moonshots diversify the business. When you are as big as Google, market share is important, but diversity is important for a few reasons. First, growth rates for existing businesses can flatten out. To sustain growth, Google needs to diversity into new high growth businesses. Second, it minimizes risk. By not putting all of its eggs in one basket, Google can be prepared for the worst. Lastly, Wall Street doesn't like surprises; a diversified portfolio can moderate volatility in Google's business.

Three, moonshots retain employees. A common misconception is that only startups can have bold, innovative ideas. As a result, employees seeking to pursue a bold new venture often leave their employer to start their own company. Instead of enabling that myth, Google can enable its employees to create startups within the company. By supplementing their employees with money, Google can fight the misconception, retain talent and most importantly, discover future growth engines.

To conclude, Google invests so much in moonshot projects because they fit its innovative culture and makes sense economically. They also help diversify Google's business. Moonshots also help to retain customers.

Chapter 19 Operations

Uber in a New City

How would you start Uber operations in a city with no precedent?

Things to Consider

- The interviewer is asking you to develop a plan.
- The phrase "with no precedent" strongly implies that you need to bring your own assumptions and knowledge to the table. In other words, you should not be wasting time asking for background information. It could be that the interviewer doesn't have it or perhaps doesn't want to reveal it to you. Revealing background information may divulge confidential information or make the interview question too easy.

Common Mistakes

- Asking the interviewer an excessive number of questions, especially when the interviewer's responses and body language strongly indicate that he or she is not going to provide additional context.

Answer

CANDIDATE: Does the city see heavy car usage?

INTERVIEWER: How would you handle either case?

CANDIDATE: Hmm, okay. I'll discuss that in a bit. What about taxi? Does the city have a lot of taxis?

INTERVIEWER: Why don't you write down solutions for all of these scenarios?

CANDIDATE: All right. I would think along these:

- **Heavy Car Usage.** If the city has a lot of car usage, it makes it easier to get Uber started. Otherwise, where are we going to get drivers? If there are not a lot of cars, then we might need to work with a local car dealership to see if we can work with them so they sell attractively priced vehicles for would-be Uber drivers.
- **Traffic.** Is there a lot of traffic? If so, I would suggest promoting things like UberPool and reducing traffic. The experience might be bad in a heavily trafficked city, so we might want to up our estimated wait time.
- **Taxi.** If there are a lot of taxis, I would check their rates and make sure we are competitive. While our core business is always to offer a better user experience than taxi rides, competitive pricing definitely helps.
- **Laws & Regulations.** We want to be aware of the laws and regulations and see how we can effectively work with them.
- **Competitors.** Do we have any competitors? Aside from Uber-like competitors, we need to consider alternatives like taxi, bus and car-sharing services like car2go.

- **Events & Local Businesses.** Work with local events and businesses to promote Uber. They will enjoy not having to provide as much parking, and we'll enjoy putting ourselves out there as a viable transportation option for people to enjoy.
- **PR.** Definitely do PR and make people know Uber is now here.
- **Digital Marketing.** We need to make sure our app is downloaded.
- **Payment.** Depending on where we are, people might use different payment platforms (e.g. mobile payments) or types of payment altogether (e.g. prepaid cards, carrier billing). We need to make sure we are adjusting to the local flavor.

To summarize, first I would make sure the barrier of entry for drivers isn't too high. If it is, we'll never get enough drivers. Then I'll price based on the competition. We then want to make sure to introduce services the market will find easy-to-use such as the most convenient ways for people to pay. Finally, I want to promote our service through multiple channels including word-of-mouth, social media ads and video ads.

INTERVIEWER: It's good that you mentioned legal requirements. What if the city says Uber drivers need special driver certification?

CANDIDATE: Special driver certification is detrimental to Uber because:

1. Makes it harder for citizens to become Uber drivers
2. Reduces driver supply
3. Reduces customer satisfaction as it becomes more difficult for riders to get paired up with drivers

As a result, I would enlist lobbyists and conduct an aggressive grassroots outreach campaign. I'll ask drivers, would-be drivers and customers to support us and petition public officials.

Uber's New Service

What new service or promo would you add that provides maximum return with minimal investment?

Things to Consider

- This is a test of your ability to come up with a clever idea.
- To increase your chance of getting something clever, brainstorm at least 10 ideas.
- To make the interviewer more receptive to your idea, demonstrate the value by explaining the necessary context: what it is, how it works and why it's unique and valuable, to Uber.

Common Mistakes

- Uninspired, ordinary ideas.
- Suggesting ideas done by Uber already.

Answer

CANDIDATE: Hmm, do I have any restrictions?

INTERVIEWER: Nope.

CANDIDATE: Can you give me some time to brainstorm?

Candidate takes one minute.

CANDIDATE: Okay, I have a few ideas:

- **Uber Funds.** You can buy Uber credits at a discount. We will have a different deal every month, and it will be capped. This would allow us to get money from them earlier, and customers will end up using Uber credits because they can't use it anywhere else. If this really kicks off, we can even expand this into a payment system.
- **Uber Points.** Every ride you take, depending on the miles, you get points. With enough points, you can redeem for Uber credits. This is good because it'll encourage users to use Uber more, and Uber credits can only be used toward Uber anyway.
- **Uber Events.** Whenever there is a huge event, we can work with them to allow for a designated spot for Uber drivers to park, drop off, and wait for customers. The event can get a cut, we can promote the event on Uber and the customers find it easier to use Uber for the event.

Most of these are targeted toward customers because I am not really worried about drivers. With enough customers, surge pricing will take care of the driver aspect.

INTERVIEWER: Why do you think Uber Funds will be popular?

CANDIDATE: A lot of services offer similar things, like Amazon or Apple. It's store credits, essentially, and if some people use Uber quite a bit anyway or plan to use it in the future, buying credits is worth it for them. It's also worth it for us, because we get their money earlier. Not only do we get that, but the users will have to use Uber to spend the credits, and I bet most people won't clear it down to 0 so that's a lot of free money, essentially.

Uber Ice Cream

Let's say we want to launch Uber ice cream for the first time. How many drivers do you need?

Things to Consider

- What is the demand?
- How many cars are needed to satisfy that demand?

Common Mistakes

- Not pausing to think before starting
- Not explaining approach to answering the question before beginning

Answer

CANDIDATE: What kind of ice cream service are you thinking of?

INTERVIEWER: What do you have in mind?

CANDIDATE: Well, I can think of at least 3 broad categories:

- Delivering ice cream to consumers, on behalf of ice cream shops like Baskin-Robbins.
- Buying, selling and deliver Uber's own ice cream brand.
- Driving ice cream trucks for businesses.

INTERVIEWER: Which one do you think is more likely?

CANDIDATE: Delivering ice cream to consumers, on behalf of ice cream shops. I don't see Uber starting the entire ice cream pipeline.

INTERVIEWER: Yeah, let's go with that one.

CANDIDATE: If we are launching this product for the first time, it makes sense that we are only working with certain ice cream shops, maybe Baskin-Robbins. Baskin-Robbins have a lot of flavors, and you can do some crazy combinations. Since it takes time to concoct, we probably need at least an hour to deliver them.

INTERVIEWER: Okay.

CANDIDATE: We are probably going to deliver within a 10-mile radius, and Uber charges about $1.20 per mile. We are talking an average of 5 miles, which is a $6 driving fee. We should probably charge an special ice cream delivery fee. And drivers probably expect a tip. So my best guess is around $8: a $6 driving fee plus a $2 ice cream delivery fee. ($2 is consistent with what pizza shops charge for delivery.) We should also expect about a $5 average tips from customers.

In total, that's $13 more on average for Uber delivered ice cream. It's hard for me to imagine significant adoption for this, so I'll assume around 2 to 4% of the existing user base. I'll be generous and go with the higher 4% number in my calculations.

To continue my estimate, I'll assume the following:

- Baskin-Robbins opens from 10 AM to 10 PM. That's a 12 hour delivery window.
- I live in San Francisco, so there is about 1 million people here.

Let's put this all in a formula:

Calculating Drivers Needed:

$$Drivers\ Needed = \frac{Population * Adoption\ Rate}{\frac{Shop\ Hours}{Delivery\ Time}}$$

$$Drivers\ Needed = \frac{1\ million * 4\%}{\frac{12}{1}}$$

$$Drivers\ Needed = \sim 3,300$$

I would say we need around 3,300 drivers.

100 Drivers

100 Uber drivers show up at the office to complain. How do you manage the situation?

Things to Consider

- Listen to the complaint.
- Demonstrate empathy.
- Investigate the situation.
- Implement long-term remedies.
- Communicate throughout the process.
- For more details, refer to the Dealing with PR Disasters chapter in *Rise Above the Noise*.

Common Mistakes

- Oversimplifying the solution by saying apologizing is the solution.

Answer

CANDIDATE: What kind of complaints are they having?

INTERVIEWER: What kind of complaints do you think they might have?

CANDIDATE: I can think of several, so let me address them all and my solutions:

- **Pay is too low.** According to research, Uber drivers actually make more per hour than every other type of driver, including taxi and bus.
- **Uber cut is too high.** Same response as above.
- **No tipping.** Same response as above. Also, it's a cashless, seamless transaction. If we add this, it makes it hard for the user. Riders like to choose their tip amount. Some tip just $1. Others tip $5. This is a lot for a customer to think about, especially if they're just trying to get to their destination. By introducing friction into the process, that means fewer people are willing to use Uber, which means less money.
- **Arbitrary penalties.** We try to be very clear on this. Ask "What exact problem are you having?" and then address their problem.
- **Too many drivers.** Yes, but let say you are a rider and you are picking someone up. Would you rather pick up someone who is really good or someone who is not so good? That's why we have a rating system. If you provide a better user experience, riders will come flocking to you. I have to be a bit more tactful here because I don't want to make it seem like I am saying that a specific driver provides a bad experience.
- **Have to work an inhuman number of hours to make a living.** I would show data on how Uber pays more than equivalent jobs such as working in fast food. And better yet, Uber drivers have the flexibility to choose to work when they want.
- **Can't keep track of fares and deductions.** Everything is accessible and itemized in the app. Everything is done automatically, so that it doesn't require a lot of effort from drivers.
- **They don't want to game surge pricing, but other drivers do.** Our engineers are looking into cases like this and will ban drivers who game the system. We want to make sure everyone is playing fair.

- **Accounts got stolen**. We are having our engineering team work on a solution for this as we speak. I'll promise them we will keep them updated. I'll also ask them to bring up their issues with our support team and fight for issues on their behalf.

INTERVIEWER: That's a long list. I am interested in your arbitrary penalty problem. What if a driver is complaining that, he was under the surge pricing zone but then a normal request shows up? He didn't want the request, and it ended up giving him a 10-minute ban.

CANDIDATE: I'll tell him that's a really rare scenario. I am glad he told me because I was not aware of this problem. I would tell him I want to escalate this issue and tell the engineering team to fix this. I want the engineers to add something that allow you to mark the pickup request as inappropriate and ask the system to reevaluate. If the evaluation passes, the order will be bounced back, and the user will be asked to pay surge pricing. I'll personally follow up with him after my conversation with the development team.

INTERVIEWER: What if the developers say no?

CANDIDATE: Then I'll tell him the developers do not think this feature is high priority, and it'll be some time before they can work on it. I'll promise to keep him updated.

Reacting to Taxi Riots

How would you react to cab drivers protesting Uber's existence?

Things to Consider

- Why are the cab drivers protesting: wages, competition, working conditions or something else?
- What do they want?
- What solutions will actually change behavior?

Common Mistakes

- Assuming that the problem is X when it is actually not.
- Presenting an olive branch idea and being surprised that it's not going to work.

Answer

CANDIDATE: Hmm, this is an interesting topic. Just so we are on the same page, taxi riots happen when taxi drivers feel like Uber drivers have taken too much business, and they can't fight back. So they protest to pressure the government, Uber or even the drivers to make it unlawful for Uber to operate. Taxi cab drivers feel that Uber's use of unlicensed cars to drive others around, for a fee, is illegal.

INTERVIEWER: Yes, that's basically the gist of it.

CANDIDATE: Which country or city are we talking about?

INTERVIEWER: Let's say it's Brazil.

CANDIDATE: I would propose the following:

- **Avoid certain locations.** Locations where protests are occurring may turn violent. To be on the safe side, let's avoid those areas and alert both drivers and riders.
- **Safety first.** Make sure the drivers and riders call the police if they are unsafe. Their safety is our #1 priority.
- **Pressure legally.** Deploy our lawyers and lobbyists to address the situation.
- **Make noise.** Bring the world's attention to it. Get people talking on social media. Generate peer pressure.
- **Legally abide by the rules.** Some jurisdictions have a reputation for accepting bribes. We need to resist that kind of temptation. Uber has had negative PR in the past due to aggressive business tactics; a bribery report would reinforce an unfair perception.
- **Ask for support.** Ask drivers and riders for their support. Provide contact information so that they can contact local officials and convey their displeasure. We are job creators and we are abiding the rules, why target us?
- **Provide the best service possible.** Don't let the distractions keep us from providing the best service possible.

Uber Processes

What processes do you imagine Uber has on the demand side? How about supply side?

Things to Consider

- The interviewer is testing your ability to think through key processes.
- Drawing out a process map will help you be more thoughtful while impressing the interviewer with a visual.

Common Mistakes

- Not communicating demand and supply-side processes in an organized, easy-to-follow manner.
- Missing critical yet less obvious processes, such as payment fraud detection.

Answer

CANDIDATE: For the demand side:

- Payment processes like credit cards and mobile payment.
- Fraud processes like stolen payment credentials.
- Monetization processes like ads and apps.
- Geographic specific processes both on the city, county and country level.
- Authentication processes to allow riders to easily login.
- Promotional processes to increase rider demand.

For the supply side:

- Legal processes including and not limited to taxes and driver licenses.
- Driver promotion and on-boarding processes to increase the number of new drivers.
- Drive authentication processes to allow drivers to easily login.

1000 Drivers in Four Weeks

How would you recruit 1,000 drivers in four weeks?

Things to Consider

- The interviewer is probing your ability to achieve what others believe to be impossible.
- A good answer demonstrates a willingness to embrace challenges.
- While interviewers appreciate creative ideas, feasibility of those ideas is equally important.

Common Mistakes

- Sigh loudly and other body signals that demonstrate a lack of confidence.

Answer

CANDIDATE: Here's what I'd do:

- Post on every job website, including secondary ones like Craigslist and forums. I would also recruit drivers on social media channels including Uber's Twitter and Facebook pages.
- Call up every Uber driver we have on file and start a referral program. Refer a new driver that drives at least 5 days with at least 1 ride each would merit a cash bonus.
- Run online ads on Facebook and Google, promoting the money making opportunities on Uber and the luxury of working on your own time.

INTERVIEWER: Have you thought about working with local small taxi companies that have too many drivers and not enough rides?

CANDIDATE: I have, and I don't think it's a good idea. One, they are unlikely to work with us since they view us as competitors. Two, they don't provide the same high-quality customer experience. If we service Uber customers using their cars and drivers that are unfamiliar with Uber process and standards, we could damage our own brand.

Making Uber Successful

How can you make Uber successful in your city?

Things to Consider

- Treat this question as a marketing plan or product design question, depending on the interviewer's preference.
- If it's marketing plan, use the Big Picture Framework.
- If it's product design, use the CIRCLES method.
- Resist the temptation, even if the interviewer attempts to cajole you, to answer the question from both a marketing and product design question. The scope is too large. Tackling both marketing and product elements will water down your response, making your answer less impressive.

Common Mistakes

- Not clarifying what successful means to Uber or to the interviewer.
- Not asking about the magnitude or timeframe for success.

Answer

CANDIDATE: I live in San Francisco, and Uber is already very popular here. Let me use another city as an example: Atlanta. I lived in Atlanta before. For Uber, surge pricing encourages drivers to sign-up and pick-up fares. What we need is a robust market. Since the driver incentives are in place, we just need a healthy supply of consumers. So all of my solutions target that:

- **Uber Promotions.** Do monthly promotions, such as buying Uber credits at a discount, to incentivize more customers.
- **Collaborating with Events.** Local events are big in the South, especially football and baseball. By partnering with local events, we can promote their events. In turn, they can give us a place to park, drop off and pick up customers. This thoughtful, integrated experience will encourage users to try and use Uber.
- **Uber Truck.** Southerners love driving trucks. We can provide a trucking service for buying or moving furniture.

My purpose to acculturate Uber with the city in order to provide a better experience for the customers, which in turn will promote more drivers to come.

Facebook Auto Detect

How do you think Facebook can proactively detect site abuse of community standards proactively without having the user report abuses?

Things to Consider

- First, consider what constitutes abuse of community standards.
- Second, think about how users would detect those abuses.
- Third, identify which one of those abuses can be detected by a computer.

Common Mistakes

- Spewing answers, making it hard to follow
- Not having a systematic approach, leading the candidate to miss several potential ways of detecting abuse

Answer

CANDIDATE: I am sure Facebook does have an algorithm that does this. It's most likely based on machine learning methods. I am sure Facebook can detect the following automatically:

1. Users who post the same contents over and over again, effectively spamming everyone.
2. Users who are pretending to be something or someone he or she is not. For example, impersonating Facebook personnel or a famous actor.
3. Users who are posting links or content that are not allowed by the Facebook agreement, such as phishing, porn or other malcontent.

Just from looking at these three, I would say the last category is the most common.

Obviously, this is an algorithm doing the checking, so for more serious cases, especially those involving banning of an account, it probably requires a human making the final decision. However, the algorithm can prioritize some users based on several factors:

- How long has the account been active? Does it post a lot of other "normal" content as well? How complete is the profile page?
- How often is the account posting content on a per day, per week or even per month basis?
- How long are the average posts? How many comments are they getting?

This will prioritize possible offending users for the Facebook user operation team to look at. Some first round passes will be given along with the user. For example, if a user has been a "good" user for a long time, then suddenly started to post bad content, it's likely the user account has been hacked. In this case, the team should check for this scenario. If a user is new and starts posting lots of bad content frequently, it's most likely a new account created just for this purpose and should be banned.

Improving the Help Center

Can you make suggestions how to improve the Help Center for Facebook?

Things to Consider

- Approach this as a product design question.
- Use the CIRCLES Method.
- Think hard about pain points and frustrations along with key metrics that the help team would like to optimize such as satisfaction and decreases in support tickets.

Common Mistakes

- Suggesting magical solutions, like the omnipotent support chat bot or the mindreading support recommendation algorithm, without explaining the details

Answer

CANDIDATE: Are we talking about the desktop version or the mobile version?

INTERVIEWER: Let say the desktop version.

CANDIDATE: The Help Center is when users come to Facebook for help. The whole point is to allow the user to be able to find help in the fastest way possible and not feel helpless. Just thinking about the Help Center, I can see three points of improvements:

- **No Live Chat or Email.** While we do want users to use the FAQ and self-help sections first, we do want to provide live chat or email as a last ditch effort. Both of these connect the user with an actual person, which could ease a lot of the frustrations of feeling helpless.
- **Too Many Sections.** The first page shows 10+ sections on the left and then a bunch of more selections on the bottom. This is a lot for a user to take in. When someone comes for help, they are already feeling helpless. When we make this harder by listing all these sections, we are telling them this is complicated and you'll take forever to find it.
- **Language Selection.** The language selection right now doesn't feel like a selection. It would be better to add a down arrow or some other sort of symbol to make it look selectable. Facebook services a lot of users in different countries and thus different languages. I am sure it currently shows the language your browser sets as default, but this should still be visible.

INTERVIEWER: Wouldn't adding live chat or email cause most users to use those instead of reading through the FAQ and finding help on their own? That would add a lot of pressure to us in terms of customer service.

CANDIDATE: I would do user testing on this, and I have a feeling Facebook might already have. But to me, I feel like people who are already here on the Help Center are already trying to self-help. They are more willing to search for an answer on their own first before they give up and try another route. So I don't think the impact will be exactly 1:1. I am sure it'll add some pressure, but I'll need to see data to make sure that is true or not.

Supply Chain Challenges

Describe how Apple's supply chain works. What challenges do we face on a day-to-day basis?

Things to Consider

How does Apple accurately predict vendor performance, such as ability to meet production targets and maintain quality standards, given that Apple's specifications are often unique?

Common Mistakes

Missing out on any of the most common supply chain challenges including:

- Challenges in forecasting customer demand
- Meeting customer expectations around quality and service
- Rising transportation costs
- Global competition
- Rising commodity prices
- Growing customer requirements
- Financial fluctuations like foreign currency risk
- Challenges with recruiting and retaining talent
- Long lead times
- Executive mandates to cut costs
- Inability to deal with complexity effectively

Answer

CANDIDATE: I would imagine Apple works with a lot of hardware manufacturers for iPhones, iPads, and Macs. Most of these are probably in Asia, and there are tons of different manufacturers. I know Foxconn is a big one, but I would imagine Apple works with a lot of different hardware manufacturers for different parts.

Here are some of the challenges I think Apple would face:

- **Syncing Up.** There will be a lot of syncing up between manufacturers. So let say the iPhone needs parts A, B, and C. If all three parts were from different manufacturers, I would imagine we would need to make sure they are synced up on production amounts and progress. If in scenarios where a certain part is needed more than the other, we would need to coordinate that too. This could happen if we need parts for repairs as well.
- **Keeping Count.** We need to make sure X number of parts are produced every day to meet with demand. This would probably change on a daily basis depending on sales figures. We would also do a lot of preemptive work, such as making sure we churn out more parts with a holiday sale coming.
- **Keeping Costs Low.** The more we produce, the less it costs. So we need to keep that in mind and work with the manufacturers. I would imagine most manufacturers discuss the price and sign it in the contract. But there could be daily changes too.
- **Delivery.** We need to make sure our parts/products are delivered to the right places (manufacturers to manufacturers, manufacturers to retail, retail to retail).

- **Debug and Test.** We might need to fly our engineers to specific manufacturers to debug and/or test.
- **Supplying.** We would need to know how many products we need to supply to retailers in different regions. Some regions might have a sale and some might not, causing a shift in demands. We might also need to ship parts for repairs, unless everything is shipped to somewhere for repair, which doesn't seem so. Apple Stores can always do light repairs and have their own spare parts lying around for the easy fixes.

Amazon Robot Picker

An Amazon Robot Picker requires a special fastener produced by a Japanese company. The end-to-end production of the special fastener comprises of five different stations summarized below.

Which station is the bottleneck in the process? And what is the capacity of the assembly line, in units per hour?

- Station 1: 45 seconds of processing time

- Station 2: 30 seconds of processing time

- Station 3: 55 seconds of processing time

- Station 4: 80 seconds of processing time

- Station 5: 20 seconds of processing time

Answer

Station capacity:

- Station 1: 60/45 = 1.33 units per minute
- Station 2: 60/30 = 2 units per minute
- Station 3: 60/55 = 1.1 units per minute
- Station 4: 60/80 = 0.75 units per minute
- Station 5: 60/20 = 3 units per minute

Station 4 is the bottleneck.

The capacity of the assembly line is equivalent to the bottleneck, so the assembly line's capacity is 0.75 units per minute.

Amazon Pick-and-Pack Utilization

Amazon's pick-and-pack operation has the following processes:

- Pick station: 7 orders per 10 minutes

- Pack station: 11 orders per 10 minutes

What is the utilization of the pack station?

Answer

Flow rate = 5 orders per minute

Utilization = Flow rate / Pack station capacity = 7 orders per 10 minutes / 11 orders per 10 minutes = 0.64

Amazon Order Wait Times

During the holiday season, Amazon customers shipped 200 orders per second.

Amazon's data science team discovered that the average number of orders waiting to be shipped was 20,650.

How long did the average Amazon order wait to be shipped?

Answer

Inventory = Flow rate * Flow time

20,650 orders = 200 orders per second * W seconds

Wait time is 103.25 seconds

Inbound Flow

You are in charge of the department that receives the product into the building and stows it to the bin where it is accessible by the department. You have two options on how to receive and stow the product. In the first option, you receive the product at 250 units per labor hour and stow it at 100 units per labor hour. You must receive it and stow it for the unit to count for production. This process results in 1% of the units stowed being incorrect. You can find and fix these errors at a rate of 20 units for labor hour with what you believe is 100% accuracy.

In the second option, you receive and stow the product in one step vs. two. The rate for this process is 80 units per labor hours for receive and stow. This process results in 1.5% of the units being stowed being incorrect. You can find and fix these errors at a rate of 20 units per hour with what you believe is 100% accuracy.

1. Which option would you select to process today's units and why?

2. Does your answer change if you are told you must fully process 100,000 units today? If yes, why?

3. Does your answer change if you are told that you have 15 associates today and you must fully produce the maximum units possible? If yes, why?

Things to Consider

- Are all the associates cross-trained to both receive and stow?
- Aside from processing time, is cost an issue?
- Is it possible to do the two steps in parallel for option 1?

Answer

CANDIDATE: Let's break these numbers down:

Method 1

It takes 1 hour to receive 250 units, then 2.5 hours to stow away these units at 100 units per hour. This takes 3.5 hours to receive and stow. This is the number of units stowed per hour:

$$\frac{250 \; units}{3.5 \; hours} = \sim 71.43 \; units \; stowed \; per \; hour$$

If we have 71 units per hour, then this is the error units per hour:

$$71 * 1\% = 0.71 \; error \; units \; per \; hour$$

Since we find and fix errors at 20 units per hour, this is the number of hours to find and fix:

$$\frac{0.71 \; error \; units}{20 \; error \; units \; per \; hour} = 0.0355 \; hours$$

Combining that with 1 hour of stowing, our real units per hour is:

$$\frac{\sim 71.43 \; units \; stowed \; per \; hour}{(1 \; hour \; of \; stowing + 0.0355 \; hours \; of \; finding \; and \; fixing)} = \sim 68.98 \; units \; per \; hour$$

Method 2

The rate is 80 units per hour. This is the number of error units per hour:

$$80 * 1.5\% = 1.2 \; error \; units \; per \; hour$$

This is the number of hours to find and fix:

$$\frac{1.2 \; error \; units}{20 \; error \; units \; per \; hour} = 0.06 \; hours$$

Combining that with 1 hour of stowing, our real units per hour is:

$$\frac{80 \; units \; stowed \; per \; hour}{(1 \; hour \; of \; stowing + 0.06 \; hours \; of \; find \; and \; fixing)} = \sim 75.47 \; units \; per \; hour$$

CANDIDATE: It doesn't matter how many units we need to process today or how many associates we have, we should always go with method 2, given the higher throughput. So to recap, I'd recommend method 2 for part 1, 2, and 3.

Last Minute Supplier Problem

Something breaks in the project at the last minute on a project, and it is from a supplier. How will you solve it?

Things to Consider

- What broke, and how important is it?
- How long will it take to fix?
- What are some alternatives to the broken part? How long will that take?
- What are the tradeoffs for the different options?

Common Mistakes

- Rushing to fix the problem without first assessing the impact, effort or consequence of not fixing the issue.
- Focusing on a long-term and not short-term solution.

Answer

CANDIDATE: This is a really broad question. Are we talking about a physical product?

INTERVIEWER: Yes.

CANDIDATE: Okay, then we are really facing with a problem where a certain part cannot be used, which halts our entire pipeline down since losing a part means the entire product is not going to work. We are basically bottlenecked. I could see several possible problems:

- Technical or mechanical problem with our own parts. In other words, a faulty design.
- Supplier problems, such as labor unrest, geopolitical instability or some other factory downtime.
- The supplier suddenly wants a higher price. Since we should have a contract, this is unlikely, but it could happen.
- Too many parts produced.
- Too few parts produced.

INTERVIEWER: Out of all of the problems, which one do you think happens most?

CANDIDATE: Technical problems followed by mechanical problems.

INTERVIEWER: So how would you address these issues?

CANDIDATE: To address each of these problems, here are some things I would consider:

- **Send out an engineer.** If it's a technical or mechanical problem with our own parts we can send out an engineer to help them fix it.
- **Alternative supplier.** If the problem is with the suppliers, we can look for alternatives. We don't want to be bottlenecked on this part and cause a delay.

- **Decision on price change.** Highly unlikely since we have a contract, but just in case, we need to gauge if the delay is worth the sudden increase in price. If so, we need to find an alternative supplier.
- **Decision on too many parts.** We can decide to make more units due to too many parts if we think the market demand will meet it (doubtful, since we should have calculated this beforehand), or we can decide to just hold on to the parts for now for spare parts. If we absolutely don't need them, then I guess we can resell them to recycle them. I would say just keep them as spare parts since we'll have to repair and make new units at some point.
- **Alternative parts.** Maybe a certain part just doesn't work or there are too few. Can we use anything else to replace the parts that are not working?

INTERVIEWER: You've suggested a good framework to think about our issues in the long-term. But what would you do in the short-term so that we can unblock production?

CANDIDATE: Here are the questions I'd ask:

- What part broke?
- How does it affect production and business results?
- How long will it take to fix? And how about cost?
- What are our different options to unblock production?
- Which is the optimal solution based on tradeoffs?

From that information, I would confer with the team and our executives to make a decision to get things back on track.

INTERVIEWER: Thank you.

Solving Supply Constraints

How would you solve supply constraints and expand the supplier base in the face of an imminent product release?

Things to Consider

- There's nothing more discouraging than strong customer demand and not having inventory to fulfill it.
- This question tests your ability to come up with creative ways to get more inventory to fill demand.

Common Mistakes

- Raising issues that won't address the supply constraint (e.g. lowering cost of critical inputs).

Answer

CANDIDATE: I am assuming you mean, what happens if we suddenly got supply blocked somehow, and we need to expand our supplier base in order to meet a product launch?

INTERVIEWER: Yes.

CANDIDATE: Okay, well when you mean supplier base, do you mean I can only solve this by adding more suppliers or is making each supplier churn out more supplies before launch a viable solution too?

INTERVIEWER: You can do anything as long as it solves the situation.

CANDIDATE: I would propose the following:

- **Change the frequency of delivery commitments.** If the supplier cannot meet 100 parts per week, could they meet 15-20 parts per day? That way we can continue shipping finished products even if it's at a lower quantity.
- **Increase supply of parts.** We can ask existing suppliers to see if they can churn out more. We need to gauge if we can hit the supplies needed before the launch to see if this is viable.
- **Use alternative parts.** If we are talking about parts, then we need to see if we can use existing parts to replace some parts that we are missing.
- **Add more suppliers.** Let see if we can get more suppliers to churn out the parts before the deadline.
- **Extend the deadline.** We may need to push the deadline back if we can't meet it.
- **Lower finished goods inventory.** Basically, we don't say anything, and the products just run out faster. People will think it's just selling really well and we can say we didn't expect this many sales and none will be the wiser.

INTERVIEWER: Interesting solutions. Which one would you recommend?

CANDIDATE: I would try to see if our existing suppliers to can churn out more. I don't think alternative parts are feasible, and pushing the deadline back is not a good idea. Finding additional suppliers is going to be difficult in a short amount of time, and quality will suffer as a result. If existing suppliers can't churn out enough, I would ask them to still try, and then just don't say anything and let the product go out of stock. Who knows, it might generate more buzz this way and increase sales in the end.

Non-Answering Supplier

What happened if the supplier does not answer your call or reply to your email? What will you do?

Things to Consider

This is largely a brainstorming exercise on different influence tactics. Here are some ideas to start:

- Reminders
- Using urgency or deadlines
- Finding another contact such as your primary contact's boss
- Activating the reciprocity principle (e.g. "I'll get your child a Michael Jordan autograph if you make my email a high priority.")

Common Mistakes

- Being too passive about the situation. That is, assuming everything is okay when it's not.
- Being too aggressive about the situation. For instance, yelling at the supplier or being unnecessarily needy.

Answer

CANDIDATE: I would first see if I could reach them through other methods, like texting, other instant messaging apps or even faxing. If it isn't time-sensitive, I could even try mailing. I would then try to see if I could reach someone else besides my primary contact in the supplier's office. My contact could be busy right now. If not or the supplier is a one-man supplier, I could drive down to the office if they are close enough or I can ask someone from the local Amazon office to do so if they are close enough. Obviously, this depends on how important this supplier is. It's unlikely I am only responsible for only one supplier, so I might ignore this supplier straight up if this isn't a very big supplier. Likewise, if this supplier's pipeline impact were minimal, I would ignore them too.

Obviously, I would love to be able to keep track of everyone and not ignore any of them in case of problems. But if I have to prioritize, I'll prioritize.

If nothing works by this point, I can confirm this supplier cannot be reached any time soon. It's time to think of alternatives. I will first see if I can find another supplier, preferably one we are already working with, who can provide us with replacements. I'll try to find one that provides replacements that are just as high qualified and around the same price and amount. I'll also see if we can find alternatives (e.g. different brand). I'll also see if I need to limit the amount of purchases by account on these products so we don't run out of stock that fast.

INTERVIEWER: What if this supply is needed for a major holiday sale or some other sort of deadline?

CANDIDATE: Besides the methods above, I would also see if we could push the deadline back if this is centerpiece for it. If not, take it out of the centerpiece and probably the whole event altogether.

Conformal Coating

Please detail the impact of conformal coating to a product's after-market serviceability.

Things to Consider

- Do you know what conformal coating is? If not, don't hesitate to ask. It's unfair to answer a question when you don't have the appropriate context.
- Based on the interviewer's description, think through how it might impact after-market serviceability.
- If the interviewer doesn't provide a description, make your best guess on what it is and ask the interviewer to confirm your understanding is correct before proceeding.

Common Mistakes

- Mumbling a response, with the goal of trying to think and talk at the same time.

Answer

CANDIDATE: Conformal coating is usually used by circuit boards to make sure they can be used in harsher environments, being able to deal with light dust, moisture, heat, and cold. It's very important because we have no idea where our users will be using our devices, so we need to cover a broad range of acceptable environments, such as desert heat vs. winter chill.

If we fail to do this, our devices may break down in harsh weather, leading customers to believe that our products are low quality and poorly made. That is something you never want associated with your brand, so it's important we have strict quality control on conformal coating.

Uninformed Decisions

If you don't have much information, how do you make decisions?

Things to Consider

- This is a test of your executive skills. That is, in the face of uncertainty, can you make decisions?
- Companies want PM leaders who do not waffle or pass the buck.
- In other words, they want PM candidates who get things done, even when the answer is not clear.

Common Mistakes

- Providing a decision-making framework that feels unsatisfying or incomplete.

Answer

CANDIDATE: It depends on the scenario, is it time sensitive?

INTERVIEWER: Let's say it is, and you have a few days to decide.

CANDIDATE: It really depends on the nature of the question, but in general I would do the following:

- **Google Search.** Let's see if I can find any information I need.
- **Surveys.** Post online surveys (at least 1000) and see if I can get a good consensus.
- **Quora.** Quora is always a nice place to ask, only if the question isn't going to expose company secrets or cause a PR sensation or something.
- **Ask Around.** I might try asking coworkers or friends at other companies. They are a good source of inspiration and feedback. Obviously, I can't divulge any company secrets.
- **Monte Carlo.** Or other similar algorithms if it's questions of this nature.

INTERVIEWER: What if, in the end, you still don't know enough?

CANDIDATE: I would be forced to make a decision based on what I know.

INTERVIEWER: What if you made a wrong decision?

CANDIDATE: It depends, right? If it's a time-critical decision, not making it will most likely cause more problems than a wrong one. If I can delay it, I'll delegate it back to buy more time to gather information. If it's something I need to make now, then I'll go on what I know.

Chapter 20 Marketing: Plans and Strategy

Challenges of Xbox

Please describe the challenges of selling and marketing Xbox.

Things to Consider

- Competition. Sony and Nintendo are committed to win, especially since they are based on the razor-and-razorblade strategy.
- Brand perception. Xbox is associated with the Microsoft brand. Microsoft is frequently not considered cool.
- Technology advances. Other technology products, such as smartphones, tablets and even smart TVs, are becoming gaming platforms.

Common Mistakes

- Not mentioning the challenges the competition's 2:1 market share lead (PlayStation 4 vs. Xbox One), especially in the context of network effects.

Answer

CANDIDATE: Are we talking about the franchise or a specific Xbox model?

INTERVIEWER: The franchise.

CANDIDATE: I think I can approach this from a few different angles.

- **Pricing:** The pricing model must have been a challenge. Although there was a lot of history in console pricing before, it had to be a risk. I know the Xbox uses the razor and razorblade model where Microsoft takes a loss on each console sold, but make returns from selling games (first party or third party). This must have financial requirements, because you are essentially burning a lot of capital before you start making revenue.
- **Public Relations:** Games, while profitable, is an industry often targeted by news such as violence in games and such. It's a risk Microsoft had to take if they wanted to step into gaming.
- **Investors & Company Direction:** It had to have been difficult to explain to the investors and the rest of the company why Microsoft is jumping into the game space. It was a different direction than what Microsoft usually did.
- **Team:** It had to build a team to make a console. This is no simple task. There are not a lot of people who can build consoles.
- **Business Relations:** Microsoft's strong suit is in its business relations with a lot of enterprises and physical distributors for its OS and software. Games are a bit different, and that must have been a challenge to establish a lot of relationships that way. Microsoft was also never into hardware much, and so those connections were also required.

- **Customers:** Customers probably were confused why Microsoft is building a console. This was a marketing problem. Microsoft had to convince gamers that it could build a console that rivals the long, established competitors in the market: Sony and Nintendo.

INTERVIEWER: That's pretty thorough. Which do you think was the hardest?

CANDIDATE: I would say business relations. It was basically every link in the ecosystem that Microsoft was unfamiliar with. It's a lot of preparation and planning. Microsoft probably had to poach a lot of people too.

Campaign for Office 365

Create a marketing campaign for Microsoft Office 365.

Things to Consider

- Define the objective first.
- Develop the value proposition for the campaign goal.
- Create the appropriate marketing materials whether it's advertising copy or marketing plan based on the objective.

Common Mistakes

- Assuming that purchase is the correct goal when it's usage. Just like a gym membership, companies may already have rights to use Office 365 but choose not to use it.

Answer

CANDIDATE: Hmm, Office 365 is a subscription-based model now, right? And if I remember correctly, it has a Home and Business edition. There are probably other tiers, but generally it's a pay per-user, per-month pricing model.

INTERVIEWER: Yes.

CANDIDATE: Okay. I imagine the biggest market for Office 365 is the enterprise market. Are you okay if I focus my analysis on enterprise?

INTERVIEWER: Sure, go for it.

CANDIDATE: I would reach out to these channels, in priority order:

- **Sales Team.** Microsoft has a large sales team with good relationships with enterprise clients. I would reach out to existing customers with an offer to upgrade to Office 365. Compared to new customers, existing customers are easier to convert. After existing clients have upgraded, we focus our sales team's efforts on getting new Office customers to purchase Office 365.
- **Online Ads.** Run online advertising campaigns, focusing on sites where enterprise decision makers frequent, such as LinkedIn.
- **Events.** Host online and in-person events to drum up interest in Office 365.
- **Public Relations.** Start churning out some articles on sites like Bloomberg, Wall Street Journal and Forbes.

In terms of positioning, I would focus on the Office 365's new features and how using the new software increases productivity. Here are some examples:

- **Real-Time Co-Authoring.** Invite others to work on the same document and see their changes in real-time.
- **Messaging.** Chat with colleagues with editing a document together.

- **OneNote Tasks**. Turn OneNotes into to-dos, including reminders.
- **PowerMap**. Turn your data into an interactive map.
- **PDF Editing**. Now have the ability to edit PDFs. Before Office applications were limited to just creating PDFs.
- **In-line email replies**. Reply to an email based on a preview snippet. No need to open the email first and then reply.
- **Offline editing**. Make changes offline on files and synchronize when one is back on the Internet, similar to Dropbox.
- **Planner**. A brand new project management tool to create plans as well as organize and assign tasks.
- **Inbox declutter**. Microsoft Outlook now organizes emails so that high-priority emails are visible first.

Azure Student Marketing

How would you market Microsoft Azure to students?

Things to Consider

- Microsoft Azure is a cloud computing service. It is best suited for student developers who are developing cloud applications, especially ASP.NET apps.
- Not all students have familiarity with ASP.NET applications, so aim for schools that include ASP.NET as part of the curriculum.
- Consider how to drive adoption of ASP.NET at schools where students do not use ASP.NET including workshops, classes and hackathons.

Common Mistakes

- Not knowing what Microsoft Azure is, especially for those without a cloud background.

Answer

CANDIDATE: Let me first think about what students do, and then their spending capacity, and then I can come up with a plan.

INTERVIEWER: Okay.

CANDIDATE: Here are a few things students do that align well with Azure:

- Build websites
- Launch websites
- Use cloud for storage
- Compute large amount of data for homework or projects
- Use tools like Visual Studio (Programmers only)
- Distribute content

We can't really expect students to spend money on these tools, as students tend to have little or no budget. Given this, I would approach from these angles:

- **Free tools.** I would advertise free tools for students. Kind of like Microsoft Spark. It would be free for students so they pick us over the others. The advantage is that they are learning everything through Microsoft tools, so when they get a job, they are going to carry that mentality with them. Companies that use Microsoft Azure will be more popular. In the end, more companies will adopt Microsoft Azure.
- **Course materials.** Release course materials to make the adaptation easier. Teachers would have resources if they want to teach it, and students would have easier time to learn the tools.
- **Industry standard.** Students have to worry about recruitment. I would market Microsoft Azure as industry standard tools, so knowing them would naturally up their chances of getting a job out of school.

INTERVIEWER: Are you proposing that we offer the service free for students?

CANDIDATE: There are some pros and cons to offering a free service to students. Starting with the cons:

1. Consumers will perceive your product as not valuable, since you are giving it away free.
2. Even if consumers find it valuable, we are unnecessarily creating an anchor where they might be willing to pay a few dollars for the service, but they definitely will not pay $25 or $50 for it.
3. We could be acquiring the wrong type of customers: the free loaders. Free loaders can be demanding and consume support resources.

Onto to the pros:

1. Encourages students to try the product when they otherwise would not have.
2. Demonstrate value for the product among those who have used it.
3. Build word-of-mouth marketing from students who have actually tried the product.

While there are good points to be made on both the pros and cons, I feel that Azure should be fighting for market and mind share. Amazon Web Services is dominating the market, and Google is competing vigorously with Google. Cloud. It is more important to get users to try our service, even free, especially considering the switching costs involved.

Launching the Chromebook

How would you launch the Chromebook?

Things to Consider

- Who is the ideal target customer?
- What is the value proposition?
- What kind of clever and creative marketing tactics will you use?

Common Mistakes

- Giving a laundry list of ideas, with limited reasoning.

Answer

CANDIDATE: Let's first think about the Chromebook. First, let's think about the ideal target market. The Chromebook requires a constant Internet connection. It is a Linux distribution, so that limits it to fairly tech-savvy people. What's good is that it's cheap; you can get a solid Chromebook for $250 the last time I checked.

INTERVIEWER: Wait, are you saying non-tech-savvy people will not like the Chromebook?

CANDIDATE: Not at all, but it's hard for someone who isn't tech-savvy to jump on a Linux distribution. While it's a thin system and it's mostly Chrome browser-based (thus the name), it is still different from the traditional Windows or Mac experience. It'll be much easier to target the tech-savvy people first.

INTERVIEWER: Okay. Keep going.

CANDIDATE: It's probably better to advertise it on websites such as Stack Overflow and other similar tech heavy sites. I feel like most tech-savvy people tend to shop online, so Amazon and sites like Newegg could also be a good source. Obviously, our own resources like YouTube and Search would be nice to use as well. As for brick-and-mortar stores, we can divert some budget to it, but I can't really see it become really effective.

INTERVIEWER: How would you launch the product itself?

CANDIDATE: Well, if it's during development, I'd do some sort of exclusive beta signup and mail a few copies to candidates. This allows us to get user feedback and creates an air of mystery around this whole thing. People are naturally curious, so this could generate some PR. I'll also contact PR channels and see if we can get some news going. Google making a laptop is a piece of interesting news in itself.

I'll go see if I can get some application developers to work on the Chromebook. We want to get them ready for the launch. Since it's a Linux distribution, there might be a lot of compatible applications already.

During launch, I'd ramp up marketing and definitely reach out to a lot of PR outlets. I want to make sure the specifications of the product are shown. I might want to offer a few different device models and make them available on multiple stores. I may also want to see if we can work with major computer selling websites to see if they can carry our product. If possible, I'd like to work with websites like Dell, but they probably won't carry the Chromebook.

After launch, I want to gauge user feedback and see what needs to be improved. Depending on how many people send in their Chromebooks for warranty repairs, I will also know what tends to break down and see if I can improve it. I'll continue to provide OS updates and release new applications. We should have some users now, so it shouldn't be that hard to bring in application developers. I'll also begin to think of designing the next model.

On the marketing side, I need to gauge where we are getting the most returns, and hit those channels. We might run out of potential users in our best channels at some point, then we need to focus on secondary channels.

Marketing Google Fiber

How would you increase adoption of Google Fiber?

Things to Consider

- Google Fiber is broadband Internet and cable TV offering. It competes with Comcast, Time Warner Cable and Charter in the United States.
- Key challenges include both awareness and limited word-of-mouth marketing.

Common Mistakes

- Giving a laundry list of marketing ideas without an accompanying strategic plan.
- Suggesting marketing tactics to drive trial without discussing awareness and trial first.

Answer

CANDIDATE: I don't know anyone with Google Fiber, so let me make sure I understand: Google Fiber is Google's broad Internet and cable TV service in the United States. Is that correct?

INTERVIEWER: That's correct.

CANDIDATE: How many subscribers does it have?

INTERVIEWER: That's not relevant to the question.

The brush off takes candidate aback.

CANDIDATE: Okay, let me brainstorm a bit for adoption ideas.

Candidate takes one minute.

CANDIDATE: I would approach it from these three directions:

- **Improve User Experience of Certain Products.** Many people use the Internet to watch YouTube, Netflix or Hulu; they also use the Internet to play online games. We can improve the user experience. YouTube is easy, but the others might require us to partner with them. I am very concerned about the news I'm hearing: last week, Comcast and other Internet service providers declared that they would start throttling Netflix and Hulu.
- **User Story.** We can run ads and PR about users who switched from other providers to Google Fiber. Comcast did the same thing vs. Dish. Since the majority of our market share will be from taking it from other providers, this is a good tactic.
- **Competitive Service.** Google Fiber is already magnitudes faster than other providers. We also need to make sure we can beat their rates as well. One of the biggest complaints is that Comcast and other providers have a monopoly on Internet, so they are allowed to charge ridiculous amount of money. If we can provide a better rate, the users will hop over.

INTERVIEWER: Which idea do you think would make the biggest impact?

CANDIDATE: I would say competitive service. I feel like this is already a strategy Google Fiber is employing, and we need to keep this up.

INTERVIEWER: It seems like a lot of your strategies are focused on grabbing market share from other competitors. Have you thought about converting new users?

CANDIDATE: I have, but most users who want Internet already have Internet. Take me for example, I'd love to use another service, but my provider is the only thing available in my area. I have no choice, which is why some users have complained that these providers essentially have a monopoly. This is why I think by providing better service at a lower cost; it's easy for Google Fiber to win out in the end.

INTERVIEWER: If that's indeed true, why do you think Google Fiber hasn't just launched everywhere around the country? Why launch slowly across select regions?

CANDIDATE: I think there are multiple reasons. One, Google Fiber probably requires a lot of infrastructure setup, and also team support. This slows things down. Two, it would take some time to make back all the money spent during setup, so it's unrealistic to launch everywhere at once. Three, it's good to launch and see how we can improve our services. Even just in the US, people are vastly different state by state. What one region wants may not be applicable elsewhere. By launching slowly, we can ensure our users receive the best service, which is great for us.

Google and Teleporter

Google just invented the teleporter. Give me your go-to-market plan. Also add three features to this teleporter.

Things to Consider

- Use the Big Picture marketing framework to build your marketing plan.
- Trial usage will be a critical marketing goal.

Common Mistakes

- Providing marketing tactics only and neglecting to discuss marketing strategy, especially how the tactics tie into the strategy.
- Suggesting marketing ideas that are bland.

Answer

CANDIDATE: Can I ask some clarifying questions?

INTERVIEWER: Sure.

CANDIDATE: I am assuming the teleporter transports people yes?

INTERVIEWER: Yes, it does.

CANDIDATE: Is it more for transporting one or two people at a time or are we talking about 5-10? How big of a group are we talking about? Also, is it practical (and cost-effective) to transport packages? Is there any limit to size, weight or number for those?

INTERVIEWER: It can transport around 50 people at once. It can transport objects as well, around the same size and weight as 50 people. Number is not a limit, just the size. It's cost-effective for both cases.

CANDIDATE: Is there some sort of cool-down period for this machine? Do we also have some hard requirement (e.g., lots of power, lots of space, government licenses) for this technology?

INTERVIEWER: There is around a 10-minute cool-down period for the machine. There is no hard requirement for this.

CANDIDATE: Can this teleport things into an empty space or does it need another teleporter on the other side?

INTERVIEWER: It needs another teleporter on the other side.

CANDIDATE: Okay, thank you for all those clarifications. Can I get some time to brainstorm?

Candidate takes one minute.

CANDIDATE: I have a few marketing plans in mind:

- **Google Shipping:** This could be our own shipping company or serving our own needs for things like Google Shopping Express.
- **Google Teleport:** Basically do our own service and offer it to high-end crowds. Never commute again! We can probably test it along the same regions where we have Google Fiber. It would make it easy to manage.
- **Working with others:** We can work with other services, like local public transportation or Uber. Basically we will be doing B2B instead of B2C.

I would like to focus on one marketing plan for the 3 features. I personally like Google Shipping a lot, because I know Google is competing with Amazon on all fronts, and this would really hit their core service.

INTERVIEWER: That's a good thought. Let's go with Google Shipping then.

CANDIDATE: Let me brainstorm these 3 features.

Candidate takes one minute.

CANDIDATE:

- **Instant Delivery:** Instantly deliver something to someone's front door or even his hands! Adds that special touch. Going to have to charge extra for this service.
- **Mini Transport:** A smaller sized option that lets people deliver smaller objects. Let's say someone wants to deliver flowers or a book.
- **Big Delivery:** Opposite of the mini transport. The point is to deliver big packages for industry and manufacturers.

If I have to pick one feature, I would pick instant delivery. This is a teleporter, and I would say the cost is going to be more than regular shipping cost. Instant delivery is going to be something pricier, and would be a different market than Amazon's gifting option. It has a bit more elite feel to it.

Selling X on Amazon.com

Imagine you are a supplier considering an opportunity to sell your flagship product X on the Amazon.com marketplace.

What challenges would you face? And how would you overcome those challenges?

Things to Consider

- What's the expected demand forecast?
- What's the best way to fulfill and ship products?
- How would you promote the product on Amazon's merchandising pages?
- What additional promotion will you do outside of the Amazon.com marketplace?
- How would you determine the price?

Common Mistakes

- Forget about setting price or assuming that determining price is easy

Answer

CANDIDATE: Here are a few challenges and solutions that I can think of:

Challenges	Solutions
Competing products	• Make a better product • Reduce prices
Alternative products	• Make a better product • Reduce prices
Other distributors, especially when Amazon is not the exclusive distributor	• Reduce prices • Offer better service such as better return policies or faster shipping
Competing websites that sell similar, competing or alternative products that become more popular because of Amazon or are cheaper	• Price accordingly • See if we need to distribute on those websites as well
Customer discovery or the challenge of not showing up to the right customers because there are too many products on Amazon's site	• Label our products accordingly • Drive traffic to our product so more people buy, rate, and comment to increase its ranking
Low conversions because product price doesn't meet Amazon's free shipping threshold	• Price accordingly • Offer a temporary free shipping promotion
Items or descriptions might be misleading	• Vet suppliers thoroughly to ensure product quality • Create an automated system to minimize misleading errors due to manual data entry
Might get a bad reputation because of certain users rating low and causing other users to not be interested	• Make our product better • Have good customer service
Poor customer service because we have to use Amazon's customer service system	• Hire in-house customer service team to monitor feedback and complaints on Amazon

Less brand awareness because we are selling through Amazon	• Design our logo in such a way that it is memorable, and include that in our product
Might cannibalize our own sales on our website or other distribution channels	• Price accordingly • Launch marketing campaigns to promote purchases on our website or other channels
Selling through Amazon means no access to customer information, making it hard to contact customers for repeat purchases or enlist them for referral programs	• Ask customers to sign up for the manufacturer's newsletter • Ask customers to register their product to receive warranty benefits

Enticing Amazon Prime

How would you advertise to entice Amazon members to upgrade to Prime?

Things to Consider

- Develop the value proposition.
- Brainstorm several creative executions for the advertising copy to get at least one great idea.

Common Mistakes

- Not contemplating why Amazon members don't currently sign up for Prime.
- Suggesting ideas that are unlikely to convert regular Amazon customers to Prime.

Answer

CANDIDATE: To answer this question, we really need to understand why people want Prime in the first place. What problems or inconvenience does Prime fix?

- **Free Shipping.** It's really nice to get your item shipped for free. Most customers don't consider shipping to be part of the price of an item, and so anything we charge on shipping feels like we are ripping them off.
- **Fast Shipping.** Most people are not very well organized. They forget to buy something they need all the time. Two-day free shipping solves that. Want anything? Get it in two days.
- **Cheaper Deals.** This is more of an Amazon.com advantage than anything. Since most of our users are buying everything on Amazon already because it's the cheapest source, why not?
- **Other Perks.** Amazon Prime has a lot of perks with videos, games, and the Kindle, among other things.

So I would approach the customers first with their problems and how I understand them, such as the ones I mentioned before, then I would provide solutions. I would even get some sort of diagram made, where I would calculate how often someone forgets to buy something and needs to go buy it, and how much that costs them, and it ends up being more expensive and less convenient (time wasted) than a year of Amazon Prime.

Recent Marketing Campaign

What recent Apple marketing campaign have you seen, and how are they different from Apple's competitors?

Things to Consider

- The intent of this question is to show that a candidate is passionate enough about the company to research Apple's current ads before the interview. This is also a test of a candidate's marketing and advertising prowess.
- A pro and con analysis could work.
- Even better: use an ad critique framework like MOB.

Common Mistakes

- Not explaining the ad to the interviewer because the candidate assumed that the interviewer is familiar with the ad.
- Focusing on superficial differences. E.g. "Apple's ads are more fun than the competitor's" or "Apple's ads have music"

Answer

CANDIDATE: I know Apple recently had an iPhone 6 marketing campaign about "taken with the iPhone 6." I felt that was really creative and different from Apple's competitors.

One, it didn't try to talk about the features of the iPhone 6. It didn't tell me how many pixels the camera can capture or how powerful the camera is. It doesn't try to convince me of anything. It just shows me the effect.

Two, it was about us as the user. It promotes us as creators, and shows that we, too, can do these amazing things as long as we have the iPhone. That's a subtle yet powerful message. Not to mention actual people captured pictures. It must have taken Apple a lot of time to find that. It felt genuine.

This is different from other campaigns, where they try to sell you things based on how good it is or convincing you how much you need it. This doesn't do that. It tries to get to the core of what Apple stands for: creativity, and it puts us in the front seat.

Attracting Uber Drivers

How can Uber attract more effectively attract Uber drivers? And how can Uber onboard the drivers in a more measured way?

Things to Consider

- Points to attract Uber drivers: compensation, flexible work schedules and meeting new people.
- Consider the steps in hiring Uber drivers: background check (criminal and driving), vehicle check and interview.
- Consider elements of onboarding Uber drivers including training to review processes and procedures.

Common Mistakes

- Not clarifying the objective.
- Not inquiring what "measured" means.
- Not understanding what defines onboarding now and in the future.

Answer

CANDIDATE: Can I brainstorm for a bit?

Candidate takes one minute.

CANDIDATE: I have several ideas in mind:

- **Increase Users.** This will have a direct effect on the drivers. More demand means more supply. We can do this in multiple ways, such as offering free credits on new accounts, which Uber is already doing, if I remember correctly. We can also offer special promotions such as 20% off for the summer.
- **Promote Drivers.** Offer additional incentives for drivers. I am thinking of things like giving a bonus for picking up at least five passengers a day or a new rewards bonus after your first ride.
- **Expand Services.** We can offer new services, like high-end car services or even buses. This indirectly adds new users, but may also cause existing users to use Uber more or in a different way.

INTERVIEWER: Which one would you recommend?

CANDIDATE: I would say increase users. It's the most direct way to do this. More users means more demand which means drivers will get more (and we get more revenue), and would also promote new drivers if the business is lucrative. Obviously we can't overdo this.

INTERVIEWER: What do you mean by overdoing this?

CANDIDATE: The last time I checked, only 20% of smartphone users have installed Uber. I'm sure Travis wants to get 100% penetration. 20% is a long way from market saturation.

INTERVIEWER: Got it. And how about onboarding?

CANDIDATE: Yes, I've got a quick question. What do you mean by onboarding in a more measured way?

INTERVIEWER: We want to on board new drivers quickly and simply. Right now it's a very time-intensive process.

CANDIDATE: Here are a couple of ideas from the top of my head when it comes to on boarding:

- **Existing driver voucher.** Instead of an onerous background check, simply have three to five drivers we trust vouch for the driver.
- **Vehicle check via phone.** Instead of a physical vehicle check, do the vehicle check via a smartphone. The user can either submit photos or do a real-time video inspection.
- **Vehicle check via a third-party**. Rather than have Uber's general managers run their own vehicle check processes, outsource this to a local third-party such as an auto body shop.
- **Driver interview**. Instead of an in-person interview, do a Skype interview. Better yet, do an asynchronous video interview where the candidate records video responses to pre-submitted questions. This saves time since the interviewer can fast-forward and skip candidates that are obvious bad fits.

INTERVIEWER: Thanks for the ideas. Which one would you go with?

CANDIDATE: Existing driver voucher sounds risky and may have potential driver collusion, even though it can be mitigated. Vehicle check via a third-party is not bad, but it still feels costly. Vehicle check via phone and the driver interview via asynchronous video interview sound compelling. I'd recommend that Uber try those two.

Selling Azure to Uber

How would you sell Azure to Uber?

Things to Consider

- This question is really about developing a value proposition statement for Azure, focused on Uber.
- First, consider Uber's Azure needs. If there are no immediate needs, consider how the Azure can develop or uncover latent needs.
- Take your time to develop your sales pitch. Polish counts. After you've carefully considered it, then present your idea to the interviewer.

Common Mistakes

- Giving an ordinary sales pitch without customizing.

Answer

CANDIDATE: I need to think about what Uber does and how might they find our service useful. I can think of the following:

- **Storage.** Uber can store their vast amount of data on our cloud storage.
- **Big Compute.** They can utilize the compute power of our cloud servers.
- **Business Analytics.** They can use our detailed monitoring tools which make it easy to diagnose issues and take action, with minimal effort.

The hardest part, though, is convincing Uber to use our service. They have an incumbent solution that's either in-house or a competing cloud service. In fact, they're probably using Google Cloud, Google's version of Amazon Web Services, given that Google is a prominent Uber investor. We'll have to work a lot harder to convince Uber to switch – whether it's with a compelling discount or a significant subsidy of consulting services.

Presenting Facebook Ads

Let's say you have a sales call to present Facebook's ad products. What would you do?

Things to Consider

- Is there a customer need?
- Is the contact person the right decision maker?
- Does the contact person have budget to purchase? If so, what is their purchasing time frame?

Common Mistakes

- Sounding scripted.
- Ignoring the prospect's objections, which in the interview is being role-played by the interviewer.
- Overselling the product when the candidate already says yes.

Answer

CANDIDATE: I would first think about who the user is. Am I correct in assuming the user is a business owner thinking whether or not they should promote their products through Facebook Ads?

INTERVIEWER: Yes.

CANDIDATE: All right, then they are probably using or thinking about using our competitors as well, so pretty much traditional marketing (e.g. billboards, TV ads) and other ad networks (e.g. Google). Now let's think about what our customers want from ads:

- **Tracking & Attribution.** They want to know that their ads are attributed so they can track their performance and weed out the bad ones.
- **Optimized for Results.** They want their ads to be optimized toward what their goals are, which could be CPI, conversions or something else altogether.
- **Precise Targeting.** They want to be able to see the performance of their ads, and figure out what their most valuable audience is. Facebook can also target both mobile and browser.
- **Data Visualization.** They want to visualize what is going on easily instead of staring at rows of Excel sheets.
- **Audience Size.** No other network has as many active users as Facebook in one platform.
- **Contextual Ads.** Very few ad networks have as many interest groups as Facebook, so it's very possible they do poorly on certain topics and areas. Facebook has no such problem.
- **Branding.** Facebook is known to be the #1 ad network in the industry. No one can compete with us.

I would tell them Facebook provides all of these. Not only do Facebook ads allow precise targeting through interests and mobile vs. browser, it can also track every ad's performance and deliver them to you in a nice, visualized manner. Finally, Facebook allows you to optimize your ads towards certain actions.

I would then tell them how traditional marketing would not be able to deliver the same result. For one, traditional marketing can't attribute and track easily, and it definitely cannot give you any meaningful data for visualization. I would then talk about other ad networks and how not only do they not have as many users as Facebook, but also have lower quality users because they don't have enough information on the user to determine what kind of ads interest them.

INTERVIEWER: What about price? That's a very important point you skipped.

CANDIDATE: Facebook ads tend to be a bit more expensive than other ads. I didn't mention it because they'll bring it up themselves. I will then explain that our conversions and CTR are much higher, so it ends up being more cost-effective. We have so many partners that we are working with. The entire industry can vouch for us.

Attracting New Businesses

What strategies would you use to attract new business?

Things to Consider

- Who is the prospect?
- Can you reach the prospect?
- What are the prospect's needs?
- How will you attract the prospect's attention?
- How are you going to communicate your product's benefit with the prospect?
- How are you going to convey trust with the prospect?
- Have you clearly defined the next step with the prospect?

Common Mistakes

- Assuming prospects are familiar with the category.
- Using formal, officious language.
- Not coming up with a compelling value proposition.

Answer

CANDIDATE: I would first think about what new businesses need and what their current situation is. Most new businesses are going to be startups, so they'll be strapped for cash. They are focused on customer adoption, and they believe creating amazing products is the best way to do so. They don't want to be distracted with complex, expensive tools that don't work.

So here is where Facebook comes in. I would do the following:

- **Inexpensive starter plans**. Take Facebook ads for example. Maybe startups don't need more than 5-10 active campaigns at a time. So let's create a self-serve system where they pay a low cost for a fixed amount of impressions. As they grow and scale, they can pay more to not only get more impression but also get more customization and targeting options.
- **Easy setup**. We need to make tools that are fast, fluid, and intuitive to use. We need to reduce the overhead so startups don't feel like they're wasting time. This means they don't need to have a long set up time with us. We also want to easily and quickly demo our product to them.
- **Responsive support**. Stellar support is the key to happy, repeat customers. They should feel they can always reach out whenever they need something and get help.

In summary, this is my three pronged approach. Between good results and stellar service, I'm confident this approach will generate effective word-of-mouth marketing.

Product X to the Global Marketplace

What would you do to bring product X to the global marketplace?

Things to Consider

- Is there demand in the new global market?
- Is the new global market already familiar with the product?
- Do you have relationships with the local market including suppliers and regulatory bodies?

Common Mistakes

- Not considering the partner ecosystem necessary to make product X successful.
- Not considering differences in local culture may affect new market adoption.
- Not factoring in government regulations and constraints.

Answer

CANDIDATE: I would do the following:

- Understand which countries/territories/regions are the best for us to start with. This can include market share, competition, ease of entry, etc. We can't realistically bring our product to every country in one go.
- See if we need to set up offices in major regions.
- See if we need to work with local partners and have them as affiliates.
- See if there are any government or legal restrictions we need to abide by.
- See if we need to take into account the local culture or religion and modify our products accordingly.
- Check the local major conventions to promote our product.
- Check the most effective local advertising format, whether it is online or offline, and what shapes and forms and take that into account.
- Make sure we are offering the most convenient way to pay, including pre-paid cards, carrier billing, mobile payment or other forms of online payment beside what we are used to.
- See if we need to have a team of business developers, customer service, marketing, product managers or operations to target that region. We can also consider whether to have the team here or locally.

See if we need to change our pricing model and price to match the local business model.

Facebook Advertising Product in Indonesia

If you were to launch a new Facebook advertising product in Indonesia, how would you do it?

Things to Consider

- Use a framework to come across as having a comprehensive, thoughtful and organized checklist, such as the Big Picture Marketing framework.
- If you're not familiar with Indonesia, take a moment to understand the local culture.

Common Mistakes

- Reciting ordinary, boring marketing tactics.
- Focusing on tactics and ignoring marketing strategy.
- Choosing a poor positioning statement, demonstrating a lack of insight around customer segments and needs.

Answer

CANDIDATE: When launching a new Facebook product in Indonesia, here are the things I'd consider:

- **Customers**. We'll have to study Indonesian advertisers and the customers they want to influence through our advertising.
- **Culture**. We will have to keep in mind Indonesian culture including ethnic and religious norms.
- **Regulations**. There may be specific regulations on forms of advertising or what can be advertised.
- **Local presence**. I'd establish a local office so our staff can build strong, close relationships with not only advertisers but also local vendors.
- **Acceptable forms of marketing**. Depending on the local culture, certain forms of advertising may be more appropriate than others. I'd also want to research local or regional tradeshows that can help increase product adoption.
- **Market-specific payments**. I'd research acceptable forms of payment. Sometimes credit card is acceptable; other times cash or invoicing is preferred.
- **Pricing**. Indonesia is very different from Western countries like the United States or Europe. We'll have to research and adjust our pricing to what's appropriate to advertiser's budgets and advertising alternatives.
- **Staffing and employees**. Hire local employees that can speak the language, understand local customs and comprehend the industry, including customer and competitive insight.

Marketing Your Favorite Technology

Pick your favorite gadget or piece of technology. How would you market that product now?

Things to Consider

- Use the marketing funnel as a checklist to evaluate gaps for greater adoption.

Common Mistakes

- Not knowing the ideal customer.
- Cannot articulate value proposition in a succinct, memorable way.

Answer

CANDIDATE: My favorite piece of technology is the Microsoft Kinect. A companion to the Xbox video game console, the Kinect is a camera that tracks a Xbox user's body movement. With the Kinect, the user's body movement can control an Xbox and serve as user input for Xbox games. The Kinect also comes with a microphone.

When marketing the Kinect to consumers, I would focus on the following:

- **Unique and intuitive**. Users can use intuitive hand and body gestures to play games. Unlike traditional video game controllers, users don't need to learn and remember what the A, B, L1 and R1 buttons do.
- **Futuristic.** Manipulating an Xbox with one's hands feels futuristic. It's reminiscent of Tom Cruise and how he used his hands to control a computer in the movie, *The Minority Report*.
- **New, exclusive games.** Several games aren't available to play on video game consoles without Kinect.

When marketing Kinect to developers, I'd focus on:

- **New market opportunity**. There will be millions of consumers who will have Kinect-enabled video game consoles. They'll be clamoring for new Kinect titles; the first set of Kinect developers can tap a promising opportunity.
- **Microsoft's commitment to developers**. Microsoft has a strong tradition of supporting developers. They are committed to world-class developer tools like Visual Studio. They also invest millions and hire top employees to building programs that help developers learn new technologies and more quickly get their products to market.

Marketing Feature X

How would you market feature X to application developers, given you have limited time and resources?

Things to Consider

- The prompt already states the target customer, so no need to clarify with the interviewer.
- The "limited time and resources" clause is asking for the candidate to come up with clever and scrappy ideas.

Common Mistakes

- Suggesting conventional marketing ideas that require significant time and resources like a Super Bowl ad.

Answer

CANDIDATE: Did you want me to brainstorm a list of tactics? Or did you want me to think more holistically about a marketing strategy and then base my marketing tactics from that strategy?

INTERVIEWER: I like your suggestion, but since we are short on time, just brainstorm a list of tactics in the next two to three minutes.

CANDIDATE: I can think of a few ways:

- Create a referral program. Then get developers we know to refer their developer friends.
- Host an event, either online or in-person, to demo the feature and provide incentives such as free t-shirts when developers sign-up.
- Host a hackathon and award a prize for the best application that uses the new feature.
- Advertise the new feature on popular websites that developers frequent such as Stack Overflow and Reddit.
- Promote the new feature on sites that do not have advertising such as Hacker News.
- Host a developer conference to talk about the feature.
- Help job-seeking developers build their portfolio by mentoring them to build new software projects (that they can include on their resume) that use the new feature.
- Develop open source code, using the new feature, which other developers can leverage.
- Hire a developer community evangelist to reach out to influential developers, hoping that these influencers will write about the new feature on their blog.

Chapter 21 Marketing: Communications

Crisis with Press and Government

How would you manage a crisis situation with the press and government?

Things to Consider

For PR disasters, refer to the following framework featured in *Rise Above the Noise: How to Stand Out at the Marketing Interview*:

- Apologize for the mistake.
- Contact everyone who is affected by the issue.
- Investigate what is happening.
- Implement long-term remedies.
- Communicate through the process.

Common Mistakes

Responding in a corporate-sounding way, including:

- Using jargon
- Refusing to take responsibility
- Showing lack of empathy
- Not suggesting concrete next steps

Answer

CANDIDATE: It depends. Are we assuming, let's say, a certain Uber service is being deemed illegal?

INTERVIEWER: Okay, let's go with that scenario.

CANDIDATE: Okay, then. I would first get in touch with the legal team and see if this is actually true. I would also see if we can work out some sort of deal with the government to change this law (and also talk with the legal team). These would be all behind closed doors. What I would not do is respond to corruption or greed or submit to mischaracterizations. That's just not something Uber does.

Next, I'll work with the press, giving my side of the story. I want to draw attention to this. This is especially important in another country. I want the whole world's attention to be on this. If there is anything unfair and unjust, we need to make sure we tell the people. Obviously, if the government thinks something we do is illegal and the law is indeed like this, Uber will comply. However, we'll work with the government in overturning these laws. We have a legal team who can do this and we can ask for the support of our drivers and riders to ask their government to do the same.

During all of this, I want to emphasize that Uber offers the best quality service and we want to make it convenient for both Uber drivers and riders. We want to create jobs and tons of drivers depend on us. Riders are also important because we want to offer them an excellent experience that they cannot get anywhere else. Our service not only provides convenience, but also value and jobs to the local community.

Responding to Mischaracterizations

Write a media statement to respond to Uber mischaracterizations voiced in a taxi leader's newspaper op-ed.

Things to Consider

- Confront the mischaracterization head-on.
- Systematically address and reject each mischaracterization.

Common Mistakes

- Avoiding the issue.
- Being vague and unclear, giving the mischaracterization merit.

Answer

CANDIDATE: Here's the media response I would write:

The taxi leader, Lane, accused us of giving poor customer service. What the taxi leader, Lane, said about us is a bit mischaracterized. Uber has always been about customer satisfaction, which is why we pride ourselves for providing the best service possible for the lowest price. Our entire process runs on customer ratings, so our riders always get the best drivers. They can also reject poor drivers.

By cutting out the middleman, we provide a service that not only costs less, but also pays more to drivers. This spurs drivers to deliver a 5-star experience. Riders can enjoy a hassle-free ride-sharing experience.

I understand that Lane feels like Uber is taking his business away. At Uber, our goal is to not harm others. Instead, we want to deliver a good ride-sharing experience. We constantly benchmark our customer's satisfaction with others'; we want to earn and maintain our customers' trust.

If Lane and taxis' leadership want to compete, we welcome them. Competition makes us stronger. But defaming us with mischaracterizations is uncalled for.

Damage Control

Someone was killed in an Uber and the news and social media is on fire. Draft the blog post to do some damage control.

Things to Consider

- Express condolences.
- Explain the situation.

Common Mistakes

- Being defensive. For instance, "Nobody mentions the millions of Uber rides where nobody got killed. This happens once, and it suddenly becomes news."

Answer

It is with a heavy heart that I report to you the news of a 31-year old man who tragically passed away while on an Uber ride. Authorities have determined that the Uber driver was not at fault. We do want to stress how important your safety is to us.

When <victim name> got on an Uber ride last night, the Uber driver was going at 30 miles per hour on a local <street name> when a drunk driver ran a red light and hit the car from the side, killing <victim name> instantly and injuring <driver name>. We always make sure our cars are equipped with air bags, but air bags could not protect <victim name> from this collision.

We stress, again, the importance of not driving drunk and our hearts go out to both <victim name>'s family and <driver name>'s family. We've reached out to both families with our condolences and asked both if there's anything we can do. <driver name> is still under critical condition in the hospital. Uber is monitoring the situation closely and will provide updates, with the families' permission.

Letter to an Uber Driver

Write a letter to an Uber driver about anything, such as a new promo or strategies to improve their earnings.

Things to Consider

- Who is the intended audience?
- What do you want to communicate?
- What action do you want the audience to take, after reading the message?

Common Mistakes

- Messages that sound overly promotional. Examples include flowery, ornate speech or excessive use of exclamation points.

Answer

Hi Drivers,

Thanksgiving is upon us, and many of us are thinking of home. To us, you are all part of our family. We are introducing a new promotion to help you earn some extra spending cash this holiday season.

We are introducing a Thanksgiving special to allow UberPool pricing for all UberX rides. What does this mean?

- Your earnings will be unaffected by the promotion. You'll make as much per ride as you do now.
- You'll get more riders. The discounted price means more fares.

This promotion will last from November 20 12:00AM to November 27 11:59PM. An announcement will appear in the Uber app, and the promotion pricing will be calculated automatically. No extra work for you or your riders. If you have any questions, please reach out to us at driver-relations@ubercorpexample.com.

Yours,

Kia S. Sammons

Local Uber General Manager

Converting an Uber Driver

In 4 sentences or less, try to sell someone on becoming an Uber driver.

Things to Consider

- This question is testing for two things: your ability to influence others and your communication ability.
- Consider the other person's needs or pain point.
- Be clear on how being an Uber driver addresses that pain point.

Common Mistakes

- Creating a message that's focused on comparing Uber with the competition, such as being a taxi driver (e.g. "Make more when compared to being a taxi driver").
- Limiting the marketing message to a rational dollar and cents approach only (e.g. "Make X% more with Uber").

Answer

Average answer

Why don't you become an Uber driver? You can work whenever you like, get paid for driving, and drive around in your neighborhood. You earn more than the average drivers across all spectrums (e.g. taxi, bus) and you don't even need anything other than a driver's license you already have and a car you already own.

Better answer

Your loved ones deserve the best: an unforgettable party, a memorable trip or a gift of a lifetime. As an Uber driver, you can earn the extra cash to do so. Driving for Uber fits into your lifestyle: you choose the hours, and you choose the routes. Getting started is easy: use your own car and bring your driver's license.

Complaining About Advertising

What would you say to someone who complains about advertising on Amazon.com?

Things to Consider

- Who is complaining?
- What is the complaint about?
- Does the complaint have merit?

Common Mistakes

- Overreacting, such as promising to take ads down, without first understanding the situation.

Answer

CANDIDATE: It depends. Who is this person? A customer on Amazon? A client selling something on Amazon? An advertiser? Or maybe an internal employee of Amazon. It might even be an investor.

INTERVIEWER: Let say it's a customer.

CANDIDATE: I would ask them if they dislike ads because they just don't like ads in general or do they just never find ads that are relevant? If it were the former, then I would tell them I'd bring their concerns to the relevant department. If it's the latter, I'll point out that I need to work with the relevant department to make sure our ad targeting is more accurate. Either way, I'll thank him for his feedback and continual support for Amazon. If he's a really high profile user and he seems really passionate, I would give him a $20 Amazon coupon or something to make him a little less upset.

INTERVIEWER: Would you actually ask the relevant department to remove ads from Amazon?

CANDIDATE: Well, no, I wouldn't, unless an overwhelming number of customers are saying that. But the PM who is in charge of that would keep track of the data anyway. Now, did you want me to analyze whether having ads is a good or bad thing?

INTERVIEWER: Thanks for offering, but we will conclude this question since it is all the time we have.

Describing Dropbox

How would you describe Dropbox to someone technically savvy? What about your grandparents?

Things to Consider

- The first part of the question is testing your ability to communicate with engineers. The second part of the question is testing your ability to communicate technical concepts with non-technical audiences.

Common Mistakes

- Not distinguishing the technical version from the non-technical version.
- Not thinking through the intended message first, giving a response that's unnecessarily long-winded.

Answer

CANDIDATE: For the technically savvy, I would describe Dropbox as a cloud storage that allows users to synchronize their files in real time. To setup the software, users download client software first. Then, Dropbox will create a special Dropbox folder on their computer. Any files in the Dropbox folder will automatically be synchronized with Drobox's servers in the cloud.

Users can install Dropbox on multiple computers or devices. Signing in from separate devices allows them to synchronize the files to the latest version, even though users are accessing via different devices.

Users should note that there is a storage limit, based on the user's account plan. In addition, each Dropbox folder occupies space on both their local computer and mobile device as well as Dropbox's cloud servers.

INTERVIEWER: And how would you describe it a less technically knowledgeable crowd?

CANDIDATE: For the less technical, I would use the following analogy. Imagine if there's a storage service on wheels. That is, this storage service can store your valuables: jewelry, keepsakes or important legal documents. Anytime you wanted to see those valuables, a delivery person will bring your valuables to you, anywhere in the world, as long as you show valid identification upon delivery. When you are finished accessing your valuables, the delivery person will hold your valuables and store them for you.

In this case, Dropbox is a mobile storage service for electronic files: digital photos, music and files. By having Dropbox store those files, the files can be accessed on any machine, anywhere in the world. And these files will always be up-to-date with the latest changes, since any change to the file from one computer will be saved.

Summarizing Online Sales Operations

How would you summarize the performance of online sales operations to a manager with little or no technical background?

Things to Consider

- This question is testing your ability to communicate technical concepts to non-technical individuals.

Common Mistakes

- Talking generically on how one would approach it rather than using an example

Answer

CANDIDATE: Is this a manager who has all the relevant marketing and sales knowledge? He or she just doesn't know the technical side very well.

INTERVIEWER: Yes.

CANDIDATE: Then I would describe everything normally until we get to the technical part. I would use examples and analogies. Unless the specific topic or description doesn't matter for him to understand, then I wouldn't skip it just because he has no technical background.

INTERVIEWER: That's really vague. Can you give me an example?

CANDIDATE: Let say I am describing the cost of ads vs. revenue. I would relate to how when he uses Internet at home or on his phone, he needs to pay for bandwidth. We have to do the same when we display these ads. The cost comes from that.

Chapter 22 Finance

Lower Revenue in Canada

In both the US and UK, Google receives X dollars of revenue from the US per Y searches. However, in Canada, Google only gets 0.5X revenue per Y searches.

What financial analyses would you conduct to explain the revenue differential?

Things to Consider

- Consider search revenue drivers including CPC and CTR.
- The search query mix may be different. For example, a smaller portion of Canada's searches has commercial intent. "Buy flowers" is an example of a commercial search query whereas "What is the longest river in the world" is an example of an informational search query.

Common Mistakes

- Not sharing thoughts in a structured way, making it hard to follow the candidate's thoughts.

Answer

CANDIDATE: Here are some analyses that I would conduct, based on the following hypotheses:

- **Dashboard data errors**. I would start by checking if the dashboard is correct. Sometimes there are errors in the data warehouse's extract, transform and load processes, leading to false reports.
- **Differences in user population**. Perhaps Canadians are less likely to buy online vs. the US and the UK. Given the lower ROI, online retailers are less likely to bid as much for advertising. Or maybe Canadians are more aggressively using ad-blocking technologies like Adblock Plus.
- **Differences in advertiser population**. Even if consumer purchase behavior was similar, Canadian advertisers may be different. For instance, perhaps certain Canadian verticals may not be as competitive as the US or UK. This could result less competition for the same number of ad slots, leading to lower prices.
- **Differences in mobile vs. PC search share**. Typically, revenue per mobile search is less than revenue per PC search. If Canada's mobile vs. PC mix is different from the US or UK, it could explain per country differences in revenue per search.
- **Differences in operating system or browser share**. Similar argument to the previous, revenue per search can differ based on operating system (Windows vs. Mac vs. Chromebook) or browser (Chrome vs. Firefox vs. Internet Explorer. If Canada's mix is different from the US or UK, it could explain the differences.
- **Differences in the product**. Perhaps the Canadian version is different from the rest of the world. Perhaps the Canadian version has a different UI. Or maybe it has a different algorithm for determining ad placement.

INTERVIEWER: Which one of these would be the easiest to diagnose?

CANDIDATE: It really depends on what dimensions are stored in the data warehouse, but I would gather that operational data like the following would be the easiest to gather:

- Device breakdown: desktop, tablet and smartphone
- OS breakdown: Windows, Mac and Chromebook
- Browser breakdown: Chrome, Internet Explorer and Firefox

INTERVIEWER: What would be the hardest to diagnose?

CANDIDATE: Understanding changes in product, data warehouse, customer or advertiser behavior would be the most difficult. This is qualitative information that's not automatically logged in most data warehouse systems. Getting this qualitative wisdom would require multiple, time-consuming one-on-one discussions.

How Does Google Make Money?

How does Google make money?

Things to Consider

- What are Google's different revenue streams?
- Which revenue streams are inconsequential and can be ignored, for the sake of conserving limited time?

Common Mistakes

- Claiming that one is not familiar with Google's revenue streams and instead answering how they would answer the question, instead of answering the question directly.
- Discussing a few, but not all, revenue streams because one is feeling tired.
- Forgetting to give a broad overview first and then going into details.

Answer

CANDIDATE: We need to analyze Google's entire service suite and list their monetization one by one:

- **Search.** The bread and butter of Google. Search allows Google to search ads, and also power things like Analytics and AdWords.
- **YouTube.** Google's huge video service, now with streaming and original content. Monetizes through ads.
- **Gmail.** Google's popular email client. Monetizes through ads and enterprise solutions. Google Hangouts is part of this, but Hangouts makes no money.
- **Chrome.** Google's browser is the most popular in the world. Monetizes through web page suggestions, and indirectly through promotion of search, YouTube, and Gmail.
- **Google Maps.** Google's GPS. Ads for companies (logos, pictures, etc.) as well as enterprise solutions.
- **Google News.** Ads.
- **Google Play.** Taking a cut from developers, and also has Google's own apps. Also has ads. Google Play Music is also part of this, and makes money selling music (taking a cut from artists). Google Play Books is also part of this, and makes money by selling books.
- **Google Translate.** Sells its service to enterprises.
- **Google Cloud Platform.** Enterprise solution.
- **Google Shopping & Express.** Ads and selling products either by Google or by others, in which Google takes a cut.
- **Google Drive.** Enterprise solutions.
- **Google+.** Makes no money.
- **Google Ventures.** Invests and makes money through returns.
- **Nexus.** Makes money by selling phones and tablets.
- **Google Photos.** Free for consumers, but can be expanded with a monthly fee.
- **Google Offers.** Coupons and promotions.
- **Google Talk.** International calls cost money.
- **Chromebooks.** Sells.

- **Chromecast.** TV services. Makes money through monthly subscription.
- **Google Fiber.** Makes money offering an Internet service.

Google Device

A user has a Chromebook, an Android phone and a regular laptop. Which device do you think Google would want the user to use more?

Things to Consider

- Which device is likely to have the most usage during a typical user's day?
- Which device is likely to have the best monetization opportunities going forward?
- Are any monetization streams expected to shrink over time?

Common Mistakes

- Not making a choice out of fear of choosing the wrong one.

Answer: Google Device

CANDIDATE: I want them to use the Chromebook more. It's a complete Google product. Every app on it is a Google product. This means they are using a Google product 100% of the time.

An Android phone might not be a Google phone (e.g. Samsung), and they might not be using Google apps. There are a ton of third party apps, and they could have downloaded these from third party app stores or direct installs. They might not even have Google payment.

A regular laptop is the one I definitely don't want them to use. Sure, they might have Chrome and use Google Search, but they could just as well be using Microsoft Edge and Bing. Not to mention they might not even be online when using the laptop, and pretty much all of Google's product is online.

Apple's Shop-in-Shop for Best Buy

What should Apple consider before implementing a shop-in-shop store for Best Buy?

Things to Consider

- What is a shop-in-shop store? How is it different from giving a supplier a dedicated section?
- What is the estimated revenue impact?
- What is the estimated cost?

Common Mistakes

- Not wanting to answer the question due to unknown assumptions
- Insulting the interviewer by saying this is a pointless question because Apple already has a dedicated section inside Best Buy

Answer

CANDIDATE: Here are a few things I would consider:

- How many people actually go to Best Buy? If there are not a lot of people, I don't think it would be worth it.
- Best Buy is open in a lot of different places. We obviously won't be opening a store in every single one. Which one should we pick? Maybe we should soft-launch this in one state and gauge the performance before deciding to expand.
- Do people who typically visit Best Buy match people who would buy Apple products?
- What is the advantage of having our store in Best Buy as opposed to just having a store in the same location?
- How much of a cut are we giving Best Buy for having a store inside their store? What about renting the space?
- Would Best Buy even consider letting us do this? What do they get out of it?
- There might be some confusion as to where to pay. When someone buys something from our store, do they pay through us or through Best Buy's cashiers?
- I am not sure if Best Buy carries our competitors' products (e.g. Android phones). If they do, would it be a good idea for us to be next to our competitors?
- Will we also be available on their online store?

Facebook Fraud

What problems do you think Facebook faces with fraud?

Things to Consider

- What kind of fraud are we dealing with? Some possibilities include identity, payment, advertiser and publisher fraud.
- What does the fraudster have to gain by committing different types of fraud?
- What kind of fraud tactics are least likely to evade Facebook's detection team?

Common Mistakes

- Assuming that Facebook doesn't have fraud issues given that it's not an ecommerce company.

Answer

CANDIDATE: I can think of a few:

- Fake users trying to pretend they are Facebook personnel, trying to get people's identity or account password.
- Users trying to pretend to be someone they're not like a celebrity.
- Users making fake pages pretending to be a certain organization or company.
- Advertisers running ads for free, using questionable payment credentials.
- Advertisers running ads that are not advertising what they are actually selling.
- Advertisers running ads that lead to phishing sites.
- Advertisers running ads that promote banned items, like counterfeit luxury goods.
- Users trying to post content that is not allowed, like hate speech or nudity.

Xbox Live Video Purchase

Tell me all the cost of goods sold (COGS) used for an Xbox Live video purchase.

Things to Consider

- How much does Xbox pay for cloud hosting?
- How much does Xbox have to pay the content owners?
- How much does Xbox have to pay to process payment transactions?

Common Mistakes

- Incorrectly including capital expenditures such as real estate for servers.
- Incorrectly including engineers' salaries. Salaries should be classified as operating expense.

Answer

CANDIDATE: Since Microsoft owns Xbox, I code and user data to be hosted by Azure, Microsoft's in-house cloud service.

I can think of the following COGS that would scale with additional video purchases:

- **Azure Cloud Service**: this negotiated cost that scales per unit would include the appropriate processing power, utilities, labor, and real estate costs needed to host each video purchase.
- **Royalty / Licensing Fee**. Selling other people's content requires us giving them a major cut.
- **Transaction Processing Fee**. We may be getting payment through credit cards or other purchasing methods. Those incur a cost.
- **Customer Service / Call Center Costs**. This is a fixed operational expense, but it's likely that this is accounted for in COGS, especially for Software as a Service products.

Yahoo's Revenue Streams

How does Yahoo! make money? Name 4 ways.

Things to Consider

- If you think this is a trick question, then clarify with the interviewer. E.g. "Do you want me to just list 4 ways literally? Or are you asking me to analyze and optimize Yahoo's money making potential?"

Common Mistakes

- Giving up because the candidate is not familiar with Yahoo's business model.
- Pretending to know, but getting the facts wrong, hurting credibility in the process.

Answer

CANDIDATE: I can think of these:

- **Ads.** Yahoo has a lot of services that can sell ads to the user. These include things like Yahoo Search, Yahoo News, and Yahoo Map.
- **Enterprise.** Yahoo has certain products that are free for consumers and can be purchased as an enterprise solution. An example of this is Yahoo Mail.
- **Sales.** Yahoo sells some products for money. Examples of this include Yahoo's TV service and Yahoo Music.
- **Royalty and Cuts.** Yahoo has some portals that sell products owned by others for a cut. Examples of this include Yahoo Shopping and Yahoo Travel.

Decreased Operating Margin

If operating margin decreased from a year before, name some reasons why this could be happening.

Things to Consider

Here are some important financial definitions, provided by Investopedia.com:

- Operating margin = (Operating income) / (Net sales)
- Operating income = Gross income – Operating expenses – Depreciation - Amortization
    - Gross income = Revenue – Cost of goods sold
    - Operating expenses can include rent, equipment, inventory costs, marketing, payroll and R&D costs
    - Depreciation = allocating costs of a tangible asset over its useful life. Machinery and buildings are examples of tangible assets.
    - Amortization = allocating costs of an intangible asset over its useful life. Patents, trademarks and copyrights are examples of intangible assets.

Common Mistakes

- Getting financial definitions wrong
- Not asking the interviewer for definitions
- Not coming up with a significant list of why this is happening

Answer

CANDIDATE: I can think of a few:

- Average salary went down in this territory.
- It's now possible to have people to work on this remotely in another country that is cheaper in terms of cost.
- Investors are losing interest in this market, so prices went down in general.
- Economy is doing badly.
- More suppliers jumped into the market, so now everything is cheaper.
- New technology was introduced this year, thus making everything more efficiently and thus at a lower price.
- There was a new market that showed up, and so the cost of marketing is now cheaper as a result.
- A lot of companies that do the same thing lost interest and left. There is now less competition, which means cheaper operating costs.
- A lot of competitors are holding on their money because they don't think the current year is worth it.

Expense Variance

If you projected a $500M expense and the variance came in at $1M, what are some of the explanations for why that is happening? Be prepared to give more than three scenarios.

Things to Consider

- Is it a positive or negative variance?
- Did you brainstorm all potential reasons and most importantly, did you brainstorm the reasons that the interviewer is thinking of?

Common Mistakes

- Getting scared by the term "variance"
- Not mentioning that forecast could have been $1M below forecast

Answer

CANDIDATE: Here are some scenarios I can think of:

Reasons why expenses are $1M below forecasted

- Accounting mistake
- Team did not get a chance to spend all of the money it intended
- Team put budgeted an overgenerous buffer, in case actuals came in higher than expected

Reasons why expenses are $1M above forecasted

- We needed more of something than we originally thought, thus increasing our cost.
- Some of the stuff came broken, and we had to replace them.
- The price for the things we needed went up between the projection and when we purchased them.
- We forgot to calculate some of the expenses, like shipping.
- We had to give a raise or recruited new people. We didn't expect this.
- Something went wrong during this thing and we had to spend more to cover up for it.
- This took longer than expected, and so our expenses went up as a result.

Linear Regression

Can you explain to me what linear regression is?

Things to Consider

- If you're not familiar with the term, it is okay to admit it to the interviewer.
- If you are familiar with the term but not confident of your answer, take time to ponder. Then, before answering, you may consider caveating your response with, "I am familiar with the term, but I'm not a linear regression expert since I don't use regressions as often as the data scientist on my team. Let me give it my best shot…"

Common Mistakes

- Giving an answer that portrays low confidence

Answer

CANDIDATE: Linear regression takes a bunch of data and attempts to find a relationship between an independent variable (result) and dependent variables (causes).

INTERVIEWER: Can you give me an example?

CANDIDATE: Let us say you want to see if there is a relationship between a car's weight and its braking time. You may collect thousands of observations, but the relationship between the two variable may not be clear when you collect those observations.

To develop a more precise formulaic relationship between car weight and braking time, a regression will derive an equation from observation samples, using a technique called "least squares." Least squares minimizes the sum of the square of the errors between the observations and the formula. If the error is large, the correlation is weak or possibly non-existent.

And one more helpful thing to remember: a correlation does not mean causation. It just implies causation.

INTERVIEWER: Okay, thanks for the clarifying example.

Eat Local

Eat Local is a small chain of gourmet grocery stores based in Seattle, Washington. Last year, its annual revenue was $2.1M with cost of sales of $1.7M.

Eat Local keeps 11 days of inventory on average, given the perishable nature of its products.

What is the annual inventory turns? And how much inventory does Eat Local have on average?

Answer

Inventory Turns = Days in a Year / Average Inventory

Inventory Turns = 365 / 11 = 33.2

Average Inventory = Cost of Goods Sold / Inventory Turns = $1.7M / 33.2 = $51K

Corporate Income Tax

Can you describe how corporate income tax is calculated?

Things to Consider

- Start with a definition.
- Help illustrate the definition with an example.
- Use the whiteboard to increase listener comprehension.

Common Mistakes

- Giving a definition without providing an example, making it hard to illustrate.

Answer

CANDIDATE: The U.S. corporate tax rate is similar to personal taxes. The corporate tax rate varies from 15% to 35%, depending on the amount of corporate income subject to tax for the year. Let's say your corporate net income is $8,000,000, so your tax would be:

- $113,900 baseline tax for this income tax bracket, plus
- 34% of income over $335,000 and under $10,000,000. The income over $335,000 is $7,665,000.
- 34% of $7,665,000 is $2,606,100.
- So your total corporate tax is $113,900 plus $2,606,100 = $2,720,000.

There is a tax rate depending on which bracket you fall in, and you pay a separate amount for each of those brackets you fall in. In our previous example, if we had made over $10,000,000, we would be paying the portion between $335,000 and $10,000,000 at 34% and portions over $10,000,000 to the next tier of some other rate.

Chapter 23 Business Development

Car Dealer Partner Leaving

A car dealer partner wants to stop doing business with Uber. What should you do?

Things to Consider

- Ask why they want to leave.
- Explore whether Uber can address the situation.
- If the issue is money, are there non-monetary ways to address the issue?

Common Mistakes

- Not offering creative ideas to save the partnership, if desired.

Answer

CANDIDATE: I would begin by asking them why they are considering leaving. This could be due to multiple problems:

- **They want more money.** They might think their share isn't high enough, and they want out of the relationship.
- **They found a competing offer by a competitor.** A competitor has approached them with a better offer.
- **We've wronged them somehow.** Maybe they were expecting a better revenue share as users increased, and we didn't do that. Maybe our services are getting a bad rep for some reason, and it is affecting them.

Which one do you want me to focus on?

INTERVIEWER: These are all interesting reasons. Walk me through your thoughts for each one.

CANDIDATE: Okay. We first need to see how much this partner is contributing. If they are only contributing a small amount of market share, then it's something to note. Same with if they are contributing a lot. Furthermore, we need to think about precedent. If we back off to give them what they want, word will get out, and we might have to provide the same deal to other partners. This will not only affect other car dealerships in this territory, but also other branches of this car dealership in other territories. Now to solve each of those problems mentioned above:

- **They want more money.** If they have a huge market share, we can see if giving them more money will affect us negatively. I mean, if we aren't making money with the new price, we might want to reconsider. In addition, we need to take into account indirect revenue sources, such as branding or PR. We can also negotiate for things like a ladder system.
- **They found a competing offer by a competitor.** Who is this competitor? Will they be a huge threat? How much market share will our competitor gain by winning this dealership over? Will this set off a catalyst reaction and make our other partnerships leave? I would check if our contracts have any restrictions against this and see if I can get them to change their minds. If the competitor is offering a better deal, then we need to be aware of what the terms for that are and see if we need to consider those

with other partnerships. Most importantly, I would start checking if the competition has reached out to other partnerships we are working with.

- **We've wronged them somehow.** Well, we need to fix it. Apologizing for the confusion would be a good start, but obviously make sure we are actually wrong first. Figure out what the true problem is and fix it. This could be a cultural problem or it could be some simple misunderstanding. If it's a critical problem on our side, like our service getting a bad rep, that's a problem we need to fix anyway.

Recruiting Drivers in City X

How would you go about recruiting drivers? What do you think your main challenges would be in city X?

Things to Consider

- Who would you target?
- Where would you find them?
- How would you convince them to sign up?

Common Mistakes

- Not citing driver retention. According to Uber, half of its drivers quit after one year.

Answer

CANDIDATE: Which city do you have in mind?

INTERVIEWER: Let say, a major city in China.

CANDIDATE: Okay, let me talk about the challenges first:

- **Competitors.** Uber has a big competitor in China, Didi Kuaidi. Didi has a unique competitive advantage. They have strong partnerships with Alibaba and Tencent. And those partnerships have paid off. For instance, Didi has Alipay and WeChat Pay integration inside the app.
- **Payment.** I mentioned this earlier, but most people in China use Alipay or WeChat Pay, so it's hard to get in the market if we don't do the same. I know Uber has integrated Alipay lately, but it doesn't seem likely Tencent will work with us. In fact, Tencent just blocked Alipay from WeChat, the #1 mobile social app in China. This makes it hard for customers, which makes it hard for drivers.
- **Government.** While this hasn't been a problem yet, China does have the precedent of favoring local businesses over foreign ones. I am not sure how taxes work with Uber right now in China, but this could be a problem for us in getting drivers. Taxi licenses could also be another problem.

Now I'll think about solutions to each one:

- **Against Competition.** We need to offer a better service for both drivers and customers. I know Uber has tried this before and drivers cheated the system. I know Uber is winning new customers with better customer service. Uber needs to keep this up. We can also try offering Uber credits or promotions (such as winning credits based on miles you've traveled) to incentivize customers.
- **Payment Solution.** We are in an awkward situation with Alipay not going to favor one or the other since they backed Didi Kuaidi as well. We need to work with Tencent's competitors, such as Baidu, Apple and UnionPay who provide similar payment services.
- **Government Solution.** We need to make sure to recruit local talent, especially in the legal department, and work with the government. We also need a clear approach on how to co-exist the current taxi licensing system.

I also have other solutions in general to help us acquire more drivers such as driver referrals. I can go into more detail if you want.

INTERVIEWER: That won't be necessary.

Incentivizing Drivers

How would you incentivize drivers to drive on a Saturday? Can you think of a way that does not cost Uber any money?

Things to Consider

- What are non-monetary reasons for driving? (Hint: Avoid doing household chores.)

Common Mistakes

- Blabbing in an incoherent way.
- Not having an organized framework.
- Reaching a mental block, especially with non-monetary incentives.

Answer

CANDIDATE: Can you give me some time to brainstorm?

Candidate takes one minute

CANDIDATE: I have a few ideas:

- **Event Promotions.** Find tie-ins with local events, where we can encourage participants to arrive via Uber. More demand = more supply. More drivers will show up when more riders want to Uber to events on Saturday. We could even make money from promoting events inside the app.
- **Email Campaign.** Let's promote Uber by sending emails to our riders. We can talk about how nice it is to Uber somewhere and not worry about parking. We can also tell them about special offers like luxury cars; they're perfect when one is trying to impress their date. More riders = more drivers.
- **Reaching out to Drivers.** We can show them the average number of riders asking for rides as a push notification. We can also show that Saturday can be more lucrative for them on a per hour basis. Who doesn't want to be efficient with the time they spend?

Out of the three, I like event promotions the most.

INTERVIEWER: Can you elaborate on it?

CANDIDATE: Okay, here is how it works:

- Call up local event promoters.
- As them if they would like to promote their event on the Uber app. Explain to the event promoter how much the ad might cost.
- See if the event promoter would like to give a spot for Uber drivers to easily park, pick up and drop off riders.

INTERVIEWER: When would the ad appear?

CANDIDATE: We certainly can't do it the day of the event. Riders need to plan their schedules, and they might want to invite their friends. So we might target to run the ads one to two weeks in advance.

INTERVIEWER: Is there a social media component to it?

CANDIDATE: Absolutely. Users can see the event ad, and share it with friends. That way buzz will build around the promotion, and the riders may convince them to go with them.

We can also integrate an Uber promotion with the event planner's event registration system. That is, for all the folks who register, we can suggest that they Uber to the event and save five dollars.

INTERVIEWER: Thanks for the perspective.

Identifying Content Source

Things to Consider

- Which professors are most likely to contribute learning material to an online university?
- Why would they want to contribute?

Common Mistakes

- Not knowing the challenges of creating content including developing a curriculum, giving the presentation and delivering a professional quality presentation that users expect.

Answer

CANDIDATE: The whole point of our company is to identify good sources to grab courses from so our customers find our courses both relevant and interesting. Therefore, we need to identify professors and lecturers who are good at teaching the course. This is a very broad concept, so let's define specifically what that means:

- **High Quality**. They must provide courses that are high quality. They must be relevant in today's market (e.g., programming courses are teaching languages actually used by most companies on the job).
- **Proven Track of Success.** Students from this school and/or professor must actually end up being successful after the course. For example, students who graduated from a specific professor end up working at big tech companies.
- **Course Structure.** The professor doesn't need to be funny, but courses need to keep the students' attention. I've found that strong, logical course structure can keep students' attention.
- **Research Papers.** I would see how many research papers and projects the professor has participated in to gauge his quality.

Finally, I would also check out sites like RateMyProfessors.com. I didn't list this as a primary source because the site's reviews can be biased. For example, good but tough grading professors could get low reviews. We don't want to feature only professors who give easy A's, regardless of course quality.

Strengthening Relationship

We, Coursera, are working with one institution right now that is not responding to our calls or emails. How would you strengthen that relationship?

Things to Consider

- Would the client say that you are looking out for their needs?
- Would the client say that you've been transaction or relationship-focused?
- Would they say that you're keeping in regular contact with them? Or would they say you only reach out when you have a sales-driven agenda?

Common Mistakes

- Forgetting that sometimes, clients are unresponsive because they are busy.
- Not knowing that clients may be unresponsive not because they do not have a need, but the timing is not right such as lack of budget or company-wide reorganization.

Answer

CANDIDATE: I would first see if something has happened to them. Maybe they are on a holiday or something bad happened. If not, I would try to contact my primary contact through other means, like fax or text. If not, I would see if I could find another point of contact there. If need be, and we are close enough or one of our offices is close enough, and they are important, then we can make a drive down there. That would be a good start to get them in a conversation first.

Then we can strengthen that relationship. I would talk about the benefits of Coursera to them:

- **Reach a Broader Audience.** You can reach a bigger audience, even in other countries, through Coursera.
- **No Effort Required.** They can just upload their courses online without any effort needed, since they teach their courses anyway.
- **Branding.** Make yourself better known by being on Coursera. Other prestigious institutions like Princeton and Harvard work with us.
- **Monetization.** It's an easy way to make extra cash.

I would then talk to them specifically about what they are looking for in this business relationship with Coursera and see if we can provide what they want. If they have any concerns or doubts, I also want to be there to answer them.

Business Customers in Apple Retail Stores

Why is it important for a business customer to purchase at an Apple retail store?

Things to Consider

- Come up with at least three reasons, preferably more.
- Consider Apple's cultural legacy; Steve Jobs was obsessive about controlling the end-to-end customer experience.

Common Mistakes

- Blurting out a single answer.
- Rejecting the interviewer's opinion on the matter.

Answer

CANDIDATE: There are a few reasons:

- Apple wants more control over the prospect's shopping experience. For instance, Best Buy sales representatives may not be as knowledgeable or helpful as Apple's sales representatives. Also, Best Buy may not showroom Apple's products in the manner they would like.
- They can see our other products there and might be inclined to purchase them.
- They can see Apple has the distribution and organization to open stores everywhere. It's good for branding.
- They can see Apple services a ton of other customers, both business and consumer. That's social proof.
- They know where they can ask for help if they run into issues in the future.

Relationship with School Administrators

As a Coursera business development executive, how would you manage to build relationships with school administrators?

Things to Consider

- How did you initiate contact? Warm or cold introduction?
- How did you build trust?
- How did you connect your needs with theirs?

Common Mistakes

- Mention that it's impossible to build relationships with high-level administrators without a golden rolodex.
- Assume that a single point of contact is sufficient when selling to a large organization.

Answer

CANDIDATE: I do multiple things:

- **Updates.** I would keep them updated with what's going on, especially with their own school. For example, I would share with the administrator if a professor is particularly active in using Coursera whether it's participating in course discussion or getting great reviews for their course.
- **Events.** If there are any events relevant to them, I would give them a shout out.
- **PR.** If there are any PR pieces related to their courses, I'll make sure they are aware of it.
- **Catching Up.** It's important for a business development professional to keep up to date with everyone on his or her contact list. Every once in a while, I would catch up with them over coffee or something.
- **Special Occasions.** During holidays or special events, I would send them a gift package.
- **Birthdays and Important Days.** On a personal level, I would make sure they know I remember their special days.
- **Transition.** In the unfortunate event that their primary contact is moving on, I would help facilitate a smooth transition. Nothing is worse than inheriting an awkward transition.
- **Open Door Policy.** Always be there if they have any problems or issues that they want to talk about.

Sale Not Going Through

When a sale does not go through, what is the primary reason why?

Things to Consider

- While the interviewer is asking for a single reason, it is human nature to be disappointed if the candidate doesn't mention the reason the interviewer had in mind. To protect oneself, brainstorm many reasons to increase the probability that one will correctly guess the interviewer's reason.
- Even if a candidate does not accurately guess the interviewer's reason, a large, comprehensive list of 10-15-20 items will impress the interviewer.
- To facilitate brainstorming, use prompts. That is, consider the following reasons for why a sale may not complete:
  - Customers
  - Competitors
  - Capabilities such as a non-operational website or nonsensical user interface

Common Mistakes

- Not mentioning more than one reason
- Stubbornly clinging to one's point of view and refusing to consider other alternatives

Answer

CANDIDATE: There could be multiple reasons:

- A competitor offered a better deal.
- The negotiation wasn't getting anywhere.
- They realized they don't really need this right now.
- They found it too expensive.
- The process is too cumbersome.
- They don't feel like we are a responsible company.

They were just inquiring about the price for their own purpose. They never wanted the sale to go through in the first place.

Chapter 24 Technical

100-Story Building and Two Eggs

There is a building of 100 floors. If an egg drops from the Nth floor or above, it will break. If it's dropped from any floor below, it will not break. You're given 2 eggs. Find N, while minimizing drops for the worse case.

Things to Consider

- You have two eggs.
- You can reuse eggs if they don't break.
- Knowledge of computer science concepts, such as binary search, may be helpful.

Common Mistakes

- Forgetting that there's two eggs.
- Forgetting that eggs can be reused.
- Not attempting a simple base case to get started.

Answer

CANDIDATE: Let's try a naïve approach first. Let's say I drop the first egg from every 10th floor, so 10th, 20th, 30th, 40th, etc. Let's say it breaks on the 30th floor. I know the floor is higher than the 20th but lower than the 30th. I would then start on the 21st, then 22nd, then 23rd, etc. until it breaks. In the worst case scenario, it breaks on the 99th floor, which means I must have dropped the first egg 10 times (10th -> 100th), then the second egg 9 times (91st -> 99th). So we know 19 is the answer for this approach. We want to see if we can do better.

Now, I am going to try to solve N, where N is the number of drops that is less than 19. First, we want to try dropping on the Nth floor. If it doesn't break, we now have one less drop to try, so we should go up by N – 1 floors, which would put us at N + N – 1 = 2N – 1th floor. Then we go up by N – 2 floors, and etc.

We can represent this as a formula: N + N – 1 + N – 2 + … + 1 >= 100. We say >= 100 because the total number of floors might exceed 100, but it must never be below 100 because otherwise we can't say for sure our floor is the highest without trying the 100th floor.

We can express this formula as a summation. Notice how N + 1 is N + 1, then N – 1 + 2 is N + 1, and N – 2 + 3 is N + 1? We have N numbers in total, so N/2 such pairs. We can then express it in this formula: N(N+1) / 2 >= 100.

We can then solve for the lowest value of N which should get us this number. Remember, it should also be lower than 19.

Turns out 14 is the lowest number of N that satisfies this formula. Then we have our answer. Our strategy would be:

- Nth floor: 14th
- Go up N – 1 floors: $14 + 13 = 27^{th}$
- Go up N – 2 floors: $27 + 12 = 39^{th}$
- Go up N – 3 floors: $39 + 11 = 50^{th}$
- Go up N – 4 floors: $50 + 10 = 60^{th}$
- Go up N – 5 floors: $60 + 9 = 69^{th}$
- Go up N – 6 floors: $69 + 8 = 77^{th}$
- Go up N – 7 floors: $77 + 7 = 84^{th}$
- Go up N – 8 floors: $84 + 6 = 90^{th}$
- Go up N – 9 floors: $90 + 5 = 95^{th}$
- Go up N – 10 floors: $95 + 4 = 99^{th}$. If the egg doesn't break here, we won't get our max number. Let's say it does.
- Let's try for the 95th floor all the way up to the 98th floor. It will take 4 floors.

We have a total of 14 drops. This is our answer.

Chapter 25 Product Management: General

Challenges for a PM

What are some of the challenges for a PM?

Things to Consider

Most common challenges for PMs include:

- Articulating product vision
- Convicting team on a certain course of action
- Figuring out ways to help the team do more in less time

Common Mistakes

- Complaining about unsexy tasks, such as taking notes and scheduling meetings.
- Complaining about being responsible even when the product is bad, marketing is poor, resources are limited or the engineering team is incompetent.
- Complaining about unclear executive priorities or not having enough time in the day.

Answer

CANDIDATE: The PM has a few challenges to address:

- **Convincing your team:** As a PM, you have no official authority, so if you want the team to work on your ideas you need to convince them through proven success. This can feel frustrating because you feel like you know what's best. But know that even if you have authority over other people, using it is a sign of weakness. Let your knowledge, charm and proven record of accomplishment do the talking.
- **Understanding why:** Whenever someone tells you something can't be done the way you wanted it to be or that they don't understand your ideas, you need to have empathy. You need to see from their point of view. From there, see if you can address their needs. Do so and you might convince them. Often, it's just a misunderstanding. This is why you need to dig at the why. If you don't know the real reason why, how can you fix it? This goes for both working with a team and designing a product.
- **Don't marry your ideas:** As a PM, you have a lot of ideas in your head, and not all of them will be good. This is why you work in a team and people can tell you how they feel about your ideas. Some people argue that as a PM, you are a trained professional who knows what you are doing. Engineers and designers can't possibly understand your vision. The truth is they don't need to. Every day users of your products won't care about your vision. They care about whether or not they find the product useful. When your team disagrees with you, sometimes they are actually right. Getting feedback is part of the design process. So don't be down. If an idea doesn't work, don't marry it. See if you can think of something better.

Author's Note: While this question was also covered in PM Interview Questions, *I wanted to include this alternative answer here.*

What do you like about being a PM?

What do you like about being a PM?

Things to Consider

Most PMs like the role for the following reasons:

- *Product design.* Product managers are obsessed with creating amazing products.
- *Leadership.* Product managers like the responsibility of leading teams to achieve difficult goals.
- *Managing a business.* Product managers like the end-to-end nature of building products whether it is understanding customer needs or working with engineers, marketing professional and other members of a large cross-functional team.

Common Mistakes

Emphasizing aspects that are less crucial parts of the role including:

- Training the sales team.
- Defining product pricing.
- Developing the go-to-market plan.

Answer

CANDIDATE: My favorite part of being a PM really breaks down to three points:

- **Product Design.** Designing a product from ground up that meets your users' wants is fulfilling. There are few jobs that allow for true creativity, and while you are not the designer, as a PM you do have a hand in the design. Part of the enjoyment comes from creating a design around customer needs and then convincing your team to work on it with you. It's also a great feeling when everyone is pumped about a new idea or improvement.
- **Product Improvement.** Most product development is iterative. Improvements occur after hearing customer feedback and seeing customer data. Good products are never made; they are the results of a hundred improvements. As a PM, it's your job to identify what is lacking and how to fix it. Seeing progress gives me a sense of satisfaction.
- **Impact.** There is big appeal in making a product that affects millions. Moreover, unless I'm making a bad product, it's good to know that what the team and I do make millions of people happy.

Author's Note: While this question was also covered in PM Interview Questions, *I wanted to include this alternative answer here.*

Chapter 26 Traditional

Introduction to Traditional and Behavioral Interview Questions

Although this book is focused on case questions, traditional and behavioral interview questions continue to play an important part in the tech industry's candidate evaluation process. For instance, Google's human resources department has requested its interviewers to ask more behavioral interview questions.

Amazon is even more fervid than Google about behavioral interview questions. Amazon takes a candidate's fit with its culture seriously. Amazon's culture is summarized into 14 corporate value statements called the Amazon Leadership Principles; the company tests a candidate's alignment with their Leadership Principles through behavioral interview questions.

In summary, traditional and behavioral interview questions aren't becoming extinct; they are still very much an important piece of the interview process. The last two chapters, spanning about 25 pages, will give you an opportunity to practice and compare your performance against the sample answers.

Why Should We Hire You

You have five minutes to tell me why I should hire you over the other candidates.

Things to Consider

- Interviewer is looking for your assistance to explain your nomination to their colleagues.
- Not only is important to have compelling reasons that tell the interviewer you are the best candidate for the job, but also it is necessary for you to convey it in a succinct manner, so they can easily relay it to their colleagues.

Common Mistakes

- Giving a long-winded response that is hard for the interviewer to record in their notes.
- Choosing a generic trait that is not memorable like "I work hard" or "I learn quickly."
- Giving a naïve response like "Well, you contacted me. I wasn't looking for this opportunity."

Answer

CANDIDATE: I have three reasons why.

One, I have been a PM for 3 years. I've worked with in-house, partnered, and contracted development teams in multiple countries, sometimes all at once. I've worked on projects from conception to launch to post-launch, sometimes multiple projects at once. I've launched over 10 titles in multiple international markets and grew them to be successful. I have a proven record of accomplishment.

Two, I am a very well rounded person. My startup work experience has given me the chance to wear many hats, beyond the typical set of PM responsibilities. I've worked as an engineer, QA, business development, marketing, customer service and HR. These roles have given me valuable perspective when working with others as a PM.

Three, I have a strong technical background. I have both an undergrad and graduate CS degree, and I've worked professionally as an engineer before. In a tech-driven company like Apple, working effectively with engineers starts with gaining their respect. Prior working experience as an engineer and speaking their language builds that prerequisite trust and respect.

To summarize, I am the perfect fit for this role with my proven track record, my well-roundedness and my technical background.

Tell Me About Yourself

Tell me about yourself.

Things to Consider

- "Tell me about yourself" is the most likely question you will receive at the beginning of the interview.
- This is an open-ended question that can have several interpretations. However, most interviewers want you to give them a career overview.

Common Mistakes

- Using formal, business language
- Not using specifics
- Being specific doesn't mean giving long-winded responses

Answer

As a kid, my favorite toys were rocket kits, Legos and the Apple II computer. Therefore, it wasn't a surprise that I grew up to be a computer science major at Stanford University.

While I had several software engineering internships, my true love laid in business, and I thought it made sense to join McKinsey & Company to explore my wide-ranging interests. At McKinsey, my responsibilities included data analysis, corporate valuations, process re-engineering and first-party customer research. One of my biggest accomplishments was recommending $75M annual savings for a large pharmaceutical company for 23 manufacturing facilities in South America.

In my 3rd year in the firm, I learned about the Bangladeshi social entrepreneur, Muhammad Yunus. He won the Nobel Peace Prize for founding Grameen Bank as well as pioneering microcredit and microfinance. I became passionate about the area so I joined Kiva.org. At Kiva, my responsibilities included marketing strategy, managing a content marketing team and monitoring a $5M marketing budget. One of my biggest accomplishments at Kiva was leading a partner marketing campaign with the American Red Cross, which led to over $5M in new microloans.

I've spent the last two years at the Stanford GSB, and I'm graduating in June. I am excited to be chatting with you about product marketing opportunities with Snapchat.

Before School

Tell me about yourself and what you did before school.

Things to Consider

- This is usually the first interview question, especially for soon-to-be or recent graduate.
- Many candidates mistakenly believe that this is an ice breaker question for them, when it is in fact, an icebreaker for the interviewer.
- Putting yourself the interviewer's shoes. They have a busy day; conducting a job interview is one more thing they have to deal with. Help the interviewer feel at ease with a casual, easy-going narrative that emphasizes skill keywords and highlights results, preferably in number form.

Common Mistakes

- Short responses, especially less than 30 seconds, are unsatisfying.
- Heavy usage of vague words. For example, some candidates choose to say, "I graduated from an Ivy League school with a liberal arts degree" rather than "I graduated from Harvard in Economics." The second one is much clearer and shorter.

Answer

CANDIDATE: Do you mean college?

INTERVIEWER: Yes, college.

CANDIDATE: Other than going to school, I spent a lot of time designing games on my own. It was never anything professional or serious, but I really enjoyed it. I played video games in my spare time. Whenever I played video games, I thought about how I could improve them. I didn't know I wanted to be a product manager, so this was something I had internally. I would write down what I wanted to improve, and create an experience that tried to rival the game and improve it in every way.

I also read a lot of fantasy novels. Stories and character designs interest me. The way characters develop and events fold out are some of the common reasons why people love fantasy novels. I enjoyed these aspects, but I also enjoyed the structure of the stories. As an avid reader, I devoured novel after novel. I loved intricate storylines and innovative plots. Inspired by favorite writers, I tried writing stories too. Nothing serious ever came of it, but it did help me be a better writer.

Finally, I loved playing the piano. My mother was a piano teacher, and it was only natural that I developed a taste and interest in music. My mother never expected me to be a musician. But I always felt it was important to be well rounded, both in knowledge and individual talents. And I can't help but think that my early interests from music to writing to programming nurtured that personal philosophy.

Why This Company

Why do you want to join our company?

Things to Consider

- Use the Rule of Three.
- Share your company research to reveal genuine interest in the role.

Common Mistakes

- Not sharing your company research in your answer.
- Not knowing that geographic area is an acceptable explanation for wanting to join a company

Answer

There are three main reasons why I want to join Snapchat: the Snapchat product, passion for the role and geographic location.

Product

I have been a passionate Snapchat user for the last three years. I love a few things about Snapchat:

- Short-lived sharing is addicting; it also brings me closer to those I cherish.
- Photos are faster and more powerful than text.
- Doodling, stickers and filters makes it easy and fun to express myself.
- Stories brings me closer to my friends, minute-by-minute.

My friends and family are a big part of my part of my life. It would be an honor to join a company whose goal is to bring people closer together.

Role

I am excited about the product manager role, focused on monetization. I know monetization well from my days as a Facebook iOS monetization manager. At Facebook, I was responsible for:

- Collecting requirements for new monetization features
- Building the monetization roadmap
- Working closely with engineering on feature implementation
- Managing A/B testing for monetization features
- Launch new features with an extended virtual team that spanned marketing, operations and sales

I also have extensive experience working big brands and agencies in the digital advertising space including Ogilvy & Mather, Fuel Online, and McCann Erickson.

During my tenure at Facebook, my biggest accomplishment was shipping a new behavioral targeting program, which increased Facebook's mobile revenue by 372%.

Geographic Location

Lastly, I'm looking to relocate from San Francisco to Los Angeles. My wife just started residency at UCLA Medical Center. We are hoping to be together.

What Do You Know About Us

What do you know about our company?

Things to Consider

Use the Rule of Three.

Common Mistakes

Not doing company research.

Answer

Products

- Snaps – edit photos or short videos with text, drawings and filters. Content disappears after 1 to 10 seconds.
- Stories – contribute Snaps that are semi-public.
- Discover – view short-form content from publishers like ESPN, CNN and BuzzFeed.
- Memories – save snaps and story posts.

Customers

- Taco Bell
- Coca-Cola
- Mondelez
- Beats
- Gatorade
- Burberry
- Target

Business metrics

- 100 daily active users
- 18% of all social media users use Snapchat
- 54% of Snapchat users use it daily
- 60% of Snapchat daily users that contribute content
- Time spent on Snapchat per users is 30 minutes per day
- 30% of millennials use Snapchat; whereas 11% of all Americans use Snapchat
- 35% of Snapchat users it because their content disappears
- 30% of Snapchat users use it because their parents don't
- As of spring 2016, Snapchat is the most popular social network among teenagers at 28%, followed by Instagram at 27%, Twitter at 18% and Facebook at 17%.
- Snapchat ads are viewed up to a million times per day
- Snapchat's current valuation is $20B

Challenges

- Customer adoption, beyond teenagers and young adults
- Monetization – going beyond brand advertisers and going after self-serve, performance-based advertisers

Chapter 27 Behavioral

Hardest Professional Relationship

What is the hardest professional relationship you have had?

Things to Consider

- The interviewer is testing your ability to get along with others.
- Do not dodge the question; interviewers want a genuine example.
- Do indicate what you have learned from that experience; do not allow the interviewer to conclude that you would repeat that same mistake, if you were put in a similar situation again.

Common Mistakes

- Dodging the question with a clever example that is meant to make you look good. For instance, "A boss once hated me for asking tough questions because he didn't know the answers. However, he came to accept my stellar critical thinking skills. We are now best friends, once he accepted my ability to foresee critical risks and dependencies."
- Not indicating what you have done to improve your ability to handle difficult professional relationships (aka no improvement plan).
- Not sharing with the interviewer how others perceive your ability to handle difficult professional relationships, after you have implemented your improvement plan.

Answer

CANDIDATE: The hardest professional relationship I ever had was with an artist on my team. She was a great artist by all accounts, but it felt like she took critique badly. As you know, it's sometimes a challenge to work with artists because if you feel something is off about a certain asset they've done, you have to be tactful in bringing it up.

Anyway, her name is Kay, and we had a great relationship working together in the beginning. Her skills as an artist was unmatched, and everything she did was high quality. However, whenever I had some critiques for her pieces to match what marketing or development wanted, she didn't take it very well.

I was concerned that I provided feedback the wrong way. I spoke with another artist to get his opinion about how I presented the feedback. I also asked him to observe future interactions between Kay and me. Several days later, he concluded that I didn't do anything wrong.

With that out of the picture, I tried different ways of working with her. Eventually, I realized she liked it better when I influenced her in a way that she came up with the idea herself. I guess she felt more ownership that way, and from that point on, I've always talked to her that way when sharing an idea or raising an issue. It was hard for me at first, but everyone is different. I can't expect to work with everyone the same way.

INTERVIEWER: That is an interesting story. When would you say her attitude would become a problem and not something you should indulge her with anymore?

CANDIDATE: That really depends on the makeup of the team and how important she is. It also depends on the PM. I didn't mind working with Kay at all. Not everyone is the same way.

But if I start getting complaints from other artists or even other people, then it might be something I would need to bring up with her manager and get the manager's help. I'd talk to her myself, but I wouldn't want to overstep since I do not manage Kay directly.

A Time You Failed

What is an example of a time you failed?

Things to Consider

- Use proper names for people, product and places to make your story easier to remember.
- Pay attention to the question. It is asking for an example, not a general approach to failure.
- Explain why the failure occurred.
- Indicate what you have learned from that situation and if time permits, how you approached a subsequent yet similar situation.

Common Mistakes

- Blaming others for the failure including unreasonable expectations or not pulling their weight.
- Not wanting to reveal failings, skipping the request for an example and instead, giving a general approach to failure.

Answer

CANDIDATE: As a PM, I can think of a time where I failed to address problems that led to an implosion on my product team.

During my previous job, we needed an artist for some urgent, last-minute work. So I got in contact with Paul. Paul is a good friend and an even better artist. He didn't want to work full-time, due to the long commute. So we hired him on a contract basis instead.

I introduced Paul to the team, and he quickly became good friends with everyone. He put the team and me at ease. Unfortunately, a rift started to grow between Paul and the art team.

Here's what happened: Paul innocently shared his salary to the other artists because he didn't think it was a big deal. Because Paul was a contractor, he was paid more than the full-time artists. That upset Lisa, one of the full-timers. She felt unappreciated. She worked so hard and didn't get the same pay as the new person.

The crisis between Lisa and Paul escalated, and Lisa eventually left. Paul felt guilty. He believed her departure was his fault. Now we had to find one more artist, which was frustrating because recruiting is not easy.

I felt I could have addressed this proactively with Paul. That is, he was being compensated more than others were, and he should have used discretion in sharing his salary information. Because I didn't monitor the situation, it put our team in an awkward position.

My lesson learned is to proactively address sensitive issues, closely monitor the situation and smoothly issues before they escalate. Three months later, I brought on a QA contractor, Venkat, to the team. This time, rather than put things on autopilot, I proactively addressed the salary question, asking Venkat to be judicious on how he shared information. I'm proud to announce that he's been on the team for six months. Team morale is high. Venkat integrated into the team beautifully.

Handling a Busy Situation

Describe how you would handle a busy situation where three people are waiting for help from you.

Things to Consider

- Give at least three steps, so that your proposed process sounds substantial.
- Provide an example, if time allows, demonstrating your application, mastery and ability to get a positive result from the process.
- This is a test of your prioritization skills. Saying you would "do it all" does not illustrate your prioritization abilities.

Common Mistakes

- Claiming that you would simply to do it all.
- Sharing an example that's underwhelming

Answer

CANDIDATE: Are we talking about people needing help in real life, through email, some sort of feedback system or live chat?

INTERVIEWER: Let's go with live chat.

CANDIDATE: I would make sure I reply to all of them instantly with a "Hi." This lets them know I am here now so they don't feel like they are still waiting. I would then ask them exactly what's wrong. Based on what they tell me, I would know how to prioritize them. I would prioritize them based on:

- Urgency
- How long it takes to help
- How important they are as a customer

I would ask if anyone has spare time to help with a customer. If not, I would work with the person whose requests I can finish as soon as possible while keeping the others waiting by asking them more information or with the excuse, "Let me check with another department to confirm this. Could you give me one minute?"

Then I would update them with some progress while I am trying to work through the current one until all of them are satisfied.

INTERVIEWER: What if the requests require your complete attention and you cannot multitask?

CANDIDATE: In that case, there isn't much I can do, right? I would put them in a queue and work with them one on one. I would group them the same way as before. The ones who have to wait would be unhappy, but I'll see if I can get them a discount or something to ease them.

Complex Problem

Tell me about a time when you used data to solve a complex problem.

Things to Consider

- Did you describe how you obtained the data?
- Did you summarize the top insights from your analysis?
- What decisions did you make from the data?

Common Mistakes

- Choosing an example with a simplistic data set like Google Analytics or AdWords data.
- Talked about how one analyzed data but did not:
  - Share unique, remarkable interpretations or insights
  - Recommend business decisions or follow-up analyses

Answer

CANDIDATE: During one of our mobile game launches, we had users complaining about crashes in different places of the game. At first, I asked them what kind of devices they were using, because I figured they were probably all on the same line of devices. After getting feedback from our users, I found the crashes happened across multiple devices, not just one type of device. I was stumped. Could these all be unconnected?

I asked the development team to look at each bug report. In the meantime, I dove into the data. We never tested the software across every single device; we didn't have access to thousands of different mobile devices. Therefore, the scenario was new for me.

The developers got back to me. They told me they could not replicate the crashes in our lab environment, primarily because they didn't have access to the same devices. However, they did find one interesting piece of data: the users' bug reports were related. Every scenario called upon the same UI element, a small window. They told me we'd probably have to get the devices indicated in the crash reports, so they can test and debug appropriately.

I didn't want to go on a wild goose chase. Looking for rare mobile devices could take hours, days or months. In addition, it'll cost money. So I went back to the crash reports. I discovered all of the devices were Korean Samsung devices. Moreover, all the devices have Samsung Galaxy Apps.

I shared my discovered with the developers. They dug into it and saw that Samsung's Galaxy Apps interfered with the small window UI call our app was making. We found a device in the lab with Samsung's Galaxy Apps built it, and we quickly replicated the bug. And the good news: our engineers fixed the bug and rolled out an update in four hours.

To prevent this from happening again, I created a device information reference page. We use that reference page to better pinpoint problems. The reference page allows any engineer, product manager or support team member to get information about devices. It can filter by country, default apps and services.

My boss liked how I resolved the issue, both in the short-term and long-term. He cited this specific example in the next promotion cycle, and the company promoted me from senior product manager to group product manager.

Informed Decision Making with Data

Tell me about the last time you used data to inform your decision making. How did you acquire the data? If you had to make that decision again, what would you do differently? What data would you like instead?

Things to Consider

- Most users struggle with getting access to data in the real world. Did you struggle too?
- What implications did the data show, and what decisions did you make?
- Did you regret the decision that you made?

Common Mistakes

- Not talking about the challenges of obtaining access to the data such as office politics.

Answer

CANDIDATE: One time, I acquired data on traffic sources in Southeast Asia. With this data, I prioritized which ones to integrate first, so we can optimize our incoming traffic. I acquired this data by both researching online and talking with a few PMs in other game companies who shared their data sets with me.

If I were to make the decision again, I would focus on individual country data. I would also prioritize based on the potential market share, CPI and payment habits of these countries as well.

INTERVIEWER: Did you not research this on your first pass?

CANDIDATE: I did. However, it was very time consuming to get the data, and we had a deadline. The Southeast Asian market is very fragmented with millions of jailbroken devices as well as third-party app stores.

Influencing Your Team

Describe a time where you had to influence the software or UI. What you were able to accomplish?

Things to Consider

- Take time to explain why it was so difficult to influence your stakeholders, so the listener can appreciate your persuasion skills.
- Choose your example carefully. An influence story about a back-end feature or infrastructure improvement can be boring or hard to follow. Whereas an influence story about a front-end feature may seem more enticing, but may require more effort to explain.

Common Mistakes

- Blaming the other team for not seeing it your way. This indicates low self-awareness.
- Not utilizing creative influence tactics.
- Glossing over the effort it took to influence stakeholders and making it seem that the other party changed their mind overnight.

Answer

CANDIDATE: For one of our games, we had a lower than industry standard revenue. After looking at the data, I concluded the conversion rate was fine. The true problem: average revenue per paying user.

I then drafted a plan to fix this in our next update. I convinced the team to prioritize this update for the next month. That's not the end of the story though. The real story began when after the meeting I was not completely satisfied. The fix would take a month to roll out. I was impatient. I did not want us to be in a suboptimal situation for a whole month.

I was curious to see if there was a shorter-term fix. So I went back to the data. Seven percent of our users payed for a feature that was never meant for monetization. That gave me an idea to add a similar feature as a cross-sell tactic.

I wanted to present this plan to the team, but I knew it would be hard to sell since I just got their buy-in for plan A. But I decided to give it a whirl. I contacted Hiro, our lead designer who crunches all the numbers in the game, to get him on my side before I presented this. Our team respected Hiro; having him as an ally might influence others.

I presented the idea to Hiro and explained the three benefits:

1. **Time to market**. It would be quick fix, since we are repurposing existing code.
2. **Monetization opportunity**. The feature was a cross-sell optimization, targeting users right after the purchasing cycle.
3. **Low risk**. We can test this new feature on the seven percent who are already paying for a similar feature. If the A/B test results looked good, we can then decide to roll it out to our entire audience.

Hiro liked my thinking, and he helped me convince the development team. This feature took just two days to implement. We collected three weeks of positive A/B test data and made a decision to roll it out to the rest of the players. Thanks to this feature, we increased our revenue by 10 percent. Because of our work, Hiro and I won a special founder's award the following quarter, an extra $2,000 bonus in our next paycheck.

Multiple Stakeholders

Tell me a time when you had to deal with multiple stakeholders.

Things to Consider

- Was there a sufficiently large team involved?
- Did you accidentally leave out a key stakeholder?
- Did you fail to communicate with a key stakeholder, which led to unintended consequences?

Common Mistakes

- Telling a story where the candidate is not at the center of the dilemma.
- Failing to dramatize the drama, making the situation seem insignificant.

Answer

CANDIDATE: Nine months ago, I was in charge of a new game launch where I had to deal with a European development team and a US marketing team. The dev and marketing team had different priorities for our collective group. The dev team wanted to delay the launch so they could add more game modes. The marketing team wanted to launch the new game as soon as possible; the marketing team felt that they had nothing to do.

After I had an opportunity to digest the situation, I met with both teams. I told the marketing team the reason the development team wanted to hold back, and I told the development team the reason why the marketing team wanted to launch.

Both teams were stubborn about their positions, so I made the following proposal: let's soft-launch the game now, so the marketing team would have something to do. It would also give them an opportunity to test and refine their launch plans. The development team could rely on the marketing team for soft-launch feedback, making iterative improvement before the bigger launch in three weeks.

The executives thought it was quirky that we would change launch schedules to keep the marketing team occupied. However, they liked the fact that we were getting customer input early and often. They had just brought an Agile development consultant in for training the previous week.

Providing Feedback

Give me an example of when you had to provide feedback.

Things to Consider

- Can you think of a time when you:
    - Confronted someone when others wouldn't have had courage to do so?
    - Provided feedback in an extraordinary, elegant way?

Common Mistakes

- Offering an example where the feedback was ordinary. For instance, "I suggested to my colleague that we start the meeting later so that we can accommodate colleagues joining from ten time zones away."
- Giving an example where poorly received feedback had limited or no consequences. For example, "I gave feedback that we do a cooking class, but the team voted to participate in a glassblowing class instead."

Answer

CANDIDATE: When I first worked at Dell, I was the newest member on the staff. A co-worker, who had worked at Dell for 30 years, told me that he "knew the ropes" and that I would have "wait my turn in line."

I was taken aback by his brusque approach. Unfortunately, the drama didn't end on the first day. He would never look me in the eye during meetings, and I found that he routinely left me off important emails.

I wanted to discuss the issue with him, but he never gave me the chance. I just imagined that he felt I was young and naïve. I didn't feel good being dismissed; it hurt my sense of self-worth. But ultimately, I decided to take the high road and prove myself. I worked hard, acted professionally, and learned quickly.

After about two months, he surprised me by inviting me to have coffee. He told me that he had underestimated me and that he was impressed that I tried hard to fit in and prove myself.

At that moment, I wanted to seek revenge and tell him that he was the worst person I've ever worked with. However, I decided to take the high road once again. I told him that I appreciated how he recognized my effort, and I told him that it was difficult adjusting to a new environment, especially when team members like him appeared to be unwelcoming.

He told me that he was impressed by candidness and willingness to give feedback. He later told my manager that he was impressed that I was willing to confront people and tell them bad news. He thought it was remarkable. He felt others would have scuttle the awkward feelings and choose to instead talk behind his back.

My boss shared this feedback with me and later included this positive email in my six-month performance review.

Made All Decisions

Tell me about a time when you made all the decisions for a project or task.

Things to Consider

- This question is meant to demonstrate your leadership skills.
- Many PM candidates would prefer to shift responsibility to someone else.

Common Mistakes

- Hesitating to answer because the phrase "making all the decisions," feels dictatorial, which feels unwelcome in today's team-oriented environment.
- Being perceived as a "dictator" in this response, given the question phrasing.
- Not having a happy ending. E.g. "We worked 80 hours a week for two weeks straight, but they decided to cut the project."

Answer

CANDIDATE: At my current company, the product management director resigned due to illness. As a result, I was left in charge of a poor-performing project. It didn't feel like we were making progress, and we were behind our deadlines. The executives were well aware of our issues, so they gave me and the development team an ultimatum: finish the project in two months or accept a severance package.

The development team didn't appreciate the ultimatum. After having a heart-to-heart talk with the development team, they indicated that they would be comfortable with whatever decision I made.

I felt honored to gain their trust, but I also felt a big burden on my shoulders. I was now responsible for the lives of our development team.

After considering pros and cons, I ultimately decided to finish it. We had worked on the project for four months, and I didn't feel like we were the type of team that quits. It just wouldn't be right if we didn't give it one more try.

As we pressed forward, I clarified the final deadline with my team in India. I got her feedback on how we best meet our target goals in the short time frame. From there, I prioritized all the features and cut requests that weren't essential to meeting our target goals.

I, and most of the team, worked about 80 hours a week for two months, and so did most of the team. I'm happy to say that we finished the project.

INTERVIEWER: Why did you think the project fell behind in the first place?

CANDIDATE: Here are the top reasons in my mind:

- **Unclear goals**. It wasn't terribly clear what the executives wanted us to do. One week, they wanted to increase monetization. The following week, they were preoccupied with acquiring new users.

- **Lack of vision**. The departed product management director had a groundbreaking vision for the game, but he was overruled by the executives. The executives wanted us to copy our competitors who ignited a gaming fad where they used augmented reality.
- **Lack of resources**. We originally had 5 engineers resourced to the initiative, but the executives took away three to work on a different project.

INTERVIEWER: Looking back at your decision, what would you have done if people panicked and had low morale?

CANDIDATE: I positioned the decision to go for the deadline as my recommendation. I answered any questions they had about it, but I wanted them to buy-in and own the decision.

Quick Judgment

Tell me about a time when you had to use quick judgment. What were the results?

Things to Consider

- Would most people have been indecisive if they were in your shoes?
- Was it clear that others would have asked for more time to make a decision?
- Was the result optimal, given the situation? Or did it merely indicate that you have a propensity to make rash decisions?

Common Mistakes

- Dry, boring stories.
- Gaps in the storyline.
- Unnecessarily adding extra details, primarily due to emotional baggage.

Answer

CANDIDATE: While our first game showed some success during the soft-launch, I had to make a decision regarding customer service. Traditionally, our company's product managers were in charge of the customer service. This was not sustainable in the end given our product manager's growing set of responsibilities. Therefore, I had to make a choice:

- Do I maintain the status quo?
- Or should I hire a dedicated customer service team?

The decision-making dilemma stems from the fact that it takes at least a month to recruit and another two weeks for on boarding before new team members become productive. Furthermore, if the game were unsuccessful, the newly hired customer service team would not have much to do.

After consulting with others and carefully weighing the pros and cons, I decided to hire a dedicated customer service team. In the worst-case scenario, if they do not have much to do, they can assist other team members with other tasks. In addition, to keep our costs low, I decided to hire part-time interns, not full-time employees.

I ended up hiring two customer service interns who worked 20 hours a week. I mentored them until they could stand on their own. They performed admirably, so we converted them into full-time employees when our game launched successfully. Our users loved our high service levels and more importantly, the morale of our overworked product managers improved substantially during the quarterly company poll.

Bias for Action

Tell me a time when you had a bias for action.

Things to Consider

- Hiring managers love employees who take action without being prompted. It saves them from prodding employees or having to worry about yet another thing.
- This question tests whether or not employees can get things done without prompting.
- Stronger responses show not only a candidate's initiative but also the candidate's ability to exceed expectations.

Common Mistakes

- Giving an answer that's too short. Short responses, especially those less than 30 seconds can:
  - Leaves the interviewer wanting.
  - Have you come across as inexperienced because inexperienced individuals (think new graduates) are more likely to not have much to say.

Answer

CANDIDATE: As an Amazon operations associate, I visit a lot of fulfillment centers. Over the years, I've visited fulfillment centers in Arizona, Indiana, Kentucky and Pennsylvania.

One day, I was observing incoming trucks at an Amazon fulfillment center in Indiana. I discovered that employees were unloading broken merchandise that took a lot of time to clean before the rest of the truck could be unloaded. The broken glass and boxes stopped employees from unloading the truck fully, causing more person-hours than budgeted.

I realized that the merchandise was broken because heavy boxes were sitting on top of lighter boxes. After observing the situation for a number of days, I took some pictures. I also calculated the cost of how much the company was losing. The fulfillment center was unloading trucks 30 days a year, and it required 5 additional hours to clean up for a team of 4. At $15 per hour, I found out that this was an incredible sum.

I submitted my pictures and calculations to the shift supervisor. I also proposed a new method to load the trucks. The shift supervisor asked a couple of questions and thanked me for my notes.

I was surprised that during my next visit to Seattle for the annual conference, the shift supervisor had nominated me for the employee of the quarter award. Apparently the supervisor took my recommendations, implemented them and saved $250,000 on labor.

Acknowledgments

First and foremost, thanks to my co-author, **Teng Lu**. I collaborated with him both on this book and *PM Interview Questions*. He tirelessly researched questions and prepared initial drafts. This book wouldn't have existed without him.

In addition, there's a long list of advisors who gave input and feedback along the way. I've included them below. And for those of you I've missed, the omission is unintentional.

Bobby Liu

Elisa Yuen

Jamie Hui

Joseph Watabe

Timothy Tow